Juel

Dyslexia

Dyslexia

A Cognitive Developmental Perspective

Margaret Snowling

Basil Blackwell

British Library Cataloguing in Publication Data

Snowling, Margaret
   Dyslexia: a cognitive developmental perspective.
   1. Dyslexia   2. Psycholinguistics
   3. Cognition disorders in children
   1. Title
   618.92′8553   LB1050.5

   ISBN 0–631–14432–3
   ISBN 0–631–14433–1 Pbk

Library of Congress Cataloging in Publication Data

Snowling, Margaret J.
   Dyslexia: a cognitive developmental perspective.
   Bibliography: p.
   Includes index.
   1. Dyslexia.   2. Cognition disorders in children.
I. Title. [DNLM: 1. Cognition Disorders.   2. Dyslexia. WL 340.6 S674d]
RJ496.A5S65   1987   618.92′8553   87–10376
ISBN 0–631–14432–3
ISBN 0–631–14433–1 (pbk.)

Typeset in 11 on 12½ pt Baskerville
by Opus, Oxford
Printed in Great Britain by Billing & Son Ltd, Worcester

Contents

Acknowledgements

I cannot mention here all the people who have helped me in various ways to write this book. However, I think it is important to thank the dyslexics I have worked with, who have taught me so much, particularly Danny, Caroline and Freddie. I am grateful to Uta Frith who encouraged the venture, to Peter Bryant who read an earlier version of the manuscript, and to the people I have worked closely with over the last few years namely: Nata Goulandris, Dolores Perin, Linda Pring, John Rack and Joy Stackhouse. Lastly, Chris Parker and Jackie Fowles gave me enormous support – my special thanks go to them.

1

What is dyslexia?

Reading is a complex skill yet the majority of children learn to read without difficulty. Indeed, it is puzzling when a child who in all other respects is normal has reading problems. The 'unexpected' failure of a child to acquire written language skills can be referred to as specific developmental dyslexia but it is usually called 'dyslexia' for short.

Few people who have seen a bright, well motivated child struggle over printed words would deny the existence of dyslexia. But dyslexia has defied definition. Many attempts to label children who have *specific* reading (and spelling) difficulties have been rejected, and no one description of dyslexia is universally recognized. This book will examine different approaches to the study of specific dyslexia and, by highlighting their strengths and weaknesses, we hope to arrive at an acceptable view of this developmental difficulty. Let us begin by looking at what is known as a medical model of the disorder.

The medical model

Early reports of word blindness in children emanating from medicine and allied professions led people to think of dyslexia as a 'syndrome' with associated signs and symptomatology. As recently as 1970, Critchley insisted that the diagnosis of specific developmental dyslexia was a medical responsibility and the most widely quoted definition of dyslexia is still that of the World Federation of Neurology (1968; cited by Critchley 1970). Their definition, sometimes referred to as a definition by exclusion, runs as follows:

> [Dyslexia is] a disorder manifested by difficulty in learning to read despite conventional instruction, adequate intelligence and sociocultural opportunity. It is dependent upon fundamental cognitive disabilities which are frequently of constitutional origin.

This definition has been criticized on a number of grounds, particularly because of difficulties with the terms *conventional instruction*, *adequate intelligence* and *sociocultural opportunity*. However, it still holds weight in many clinical settings.

Traditionally, in setting up guidelines for the diagnosis of dyslexia, two sets of features have been emphasized: those pertaining to the cognitive characteristics of affected individuals and those regarding their reading and spelling behaviours. Thus dyslexia, which affects three to four boys to every girl, has been associated with slow speech development, speech and language difficulties, delays in motor development and visual perceptual deficits. Other associated factors are more difficult to define but include sequencing problems (usually the inability to remember the days of the week or the months of the year is noticeable) and impairments in temporal or spatial awareness. A child with a temporal processing difficulty seems disoriented in time and may continually question whether it is morning or afternoon, while a child with a spatial problem will be confused about direction and may not appreciate left from right. Finally, many dyslexic children have inconsistent or mixed cerebral dominance. While their dominant hand is the right, they may be left-eyed, or vice versa, and there is frequently a family history of similar difficulties (Critchley and Critchley 1978). In addition, Critchley (1970) has listed among the common features of dyslexic reading and spelling: the inability to pronounce unfamiliar words with a tendency to guess wildly at their phonetic structure, a failure to realize differences between words which are similar in spelling and sound, such as pug-bud, on-no; difficulty in keeping track of the correct place when reading; problems in switching from one line of print to the next; rotations and reversals of letters; omission of phonemes and syllables; bizarre inconsistent spelling errors; and untidiness of penmanship.

It is not hard to see that there are several problems with the 'check-list' approach just outlined. How many signs or symptoms must be present before a diagnosis is made? Much more serious, where can we find good normative data? Increasingly, individual differences in language development have been noted and we know little about the development of sequencing skills, the appreciation of time or a sense of direction. Thus, to put the medical view of dyslexia into practice is difficult. Clinicians are hard-pressed to decide whether a particular constellation of difficulties is atypical given an individual's age, intellectual ability and reading level; and certainly, reading and spelling behaviours like those mentioned by Critchley cannot be counted as diagnostic. Taken in isolation these are a reflection of the level of literacy a child has attained and they say nothing about the cause of the problem. However, before dismissing the medical-syndrome view of dyslexia, it is worth considering the recent work of Miles (1983), who has tried to make an objective approach within this framework. Drawing upon some thirty years of clinical experience, Miles devised the Bangor Dyslexia Test which can be used, in conjunction with the results of a test of general ability, to decide whether or not an individual exhibits a sufficient number of 'signs' to be described as 'dyslexic'.

The Bangor test consists of twelve items. As well as determining the hand and eye dominance of the individual, testing for left/right awareness and inquiring into the family incidence of reading and spelling problems, there are also some interesting items tapping various aspects of memory. These include memory for digits (forwards and backwards), memory for sentences, tests of the ability to recite months of the year – in sequence and backwards – and arithmetic tables and to carry out mental calculations involving subtraction. In addition, individuals are asked to repeat polysyllabic words like 'preliminary' and 'statistical' and to complete a rhyming test.

Performance on the various parts of the Bangor test are scored dyslexia positive, dyslexia negative or ambiguous, according to criteria which take account of the examinee's age and are based on normative data. The total number of dyslexia-positive signs can then be calculated. While one positive sign on its own would not be significant, a critical number, depending upon the age of the indexed case, ensures diagnosis. Miles (1983) reported data from dyslexic and control subjects in three different age groups matched for intelligence, validating seven items from the test. At all age levels, children with specific reading difficulties exhibited more positive signs than normal readers (on average four or five versus two or three) and the difference was greatest amongst the older groups – the nine to eighteen year olds.

It could be argued that the Bangor test is limited in that it samples only a selected range of behaviours. However, it has two distinct advantages. First, it is theoretically motivated. In their 1981 paper, Ellis and Miles argue that dyslexia is a lexical encoding deficiency. They do not think that dyslexics have difficulty in processing visual material *per se*. Their problem emerges only when the visual information has to be labelled verbally. They postulate therefore that the difficulties which dyslexics experience are associated with the lexical (name) coding of both visual and verbal information. Thus, dyslexics have problems with short-term memory functions and also with the retrieval of stored memory traces. So, the inclusion in the Bangor test of a large number of items tapping the use of short-term memory (digit span, subtraction, repetition of sentences) and access to long-term memory (months forwards and backwards, multiplication tables) is justified. The second major advantage is that this approach gives guidelines as to when it might be appropriate to apply the diagnosis of 'dyslexia'. Miles retains the notion of a syndrome because, although the overall pattern of difficulty is similar for everyone affected, there is considerable individual variation. So, although there is room to refine an index such as this, the Bangor test illustrates a step in the necessary direction if there is to be agreement over the definition and status of dyslexia in children.

The educational viewpoint

An alternative approach rejects the notion of dyslexia as a 'syndrome' and argues instead that children who have unexpected difficulty in learning to read should be identified on these grounds alone. Teachers and educationists have never rested easy with the medical model of dyslexia. There have been a number of reasons for their dissatisfaction, the most significant being that much of the evidence on dyslexia has come from highly selected clinical samples of 'already diagnosed' dyslexic individuals. Teachers have been particularly concerned that many 'dyslexic' signs can be observed in normal readers and in slow learners. A classic example of the tendency to attribute status to an essentially normal developmental feature is the b/d reversal error, so long held to be symptomatic of dyslexia. While there may be a minority of children who have visual perceptual deficits underlying their reading failure, the consensus view is that reversal errors reflect a low level of literacy skill and do not signal dyslexia.

To avoid some of these problems, educational policy has been guided by the results of epidemiological studies. These studies sample entire populations and therefore they are not subject to referral biases. In Britain, the most influential studies have been carried out by Rutter and his colleagues (Rutter et al. 1970; Yule et al. 1974), who examined the prevalence of specific reading retardation in five different child populations. One of their main aims was to discuss whether or not it was useful to describe children with specific reading difficulties as 'dyslexic'. An initial step was to screen the entire nine- to ten-year-old population of the Isle of Wight using a test of non-verbal intelligence and a group reading test. This allowed them to determine the association between non-verbal I.Q. and reading performance in that population. Given a perfect correlation, children whose mental age is eight years would be expected to be reading at the eight-year level, children whose mental age is ten years would similarly be expected to read at the ten-year level. In practice, we can never expect such perfect association and, in the Isle of Wight studies, the correlation was about 0.6.

Taking account of the correlation between intelligence and reading skill, Rutter and his colleagues used a statistical procedure known as regression to predict for every individual in the population their expected reading age, given their chronological age and I.Q. Thus, in any individual case, predicted reading age could be compared with actual reading age attained. Two types of backward reader were distinguished on this basis. First, children whose reading was significantly below age level but, nonetheless, as predicted when their I.Q. was taken into account. Rutter and his colleagues described these children as *generally backward readers*. Most simply they can be thought of as slow learners since their reading ability is poor but so are their attainments in other areas. A second group of poor readers were children whose reading was significantly *below* the level to be expected given their age and intellectual ability. For these children there was a significant difference between their predicted and their actual reading age. Rutter et al. (1970) called them *retarded readers*. It is these children who are normally considered to be dyslexic according to the definition of the World Federation of Neurology.

To determine whether under-achievement in reading was a significant problem in the sampled populations Rutter and his colleagues examined the distribution of 'discrepancy' scores. Discrepancy scores describe the difference between predicted and actual attainments at an individual level. If discrepancy scores are normally distributed then we would expect a small proportion of under-achievement at the lower end of the curve to be mirrored by a small proportion of over-achievement at the higher end. The majority of children should be achieving at the expected level. To be precise, assuming a normal distribution of discrepancy scores, 2.28 per cent of the population should be reading two standard deviations below their predicted score (see figure 1.1). However, Rutter et al. (1970) reported a raised percentage of under-achievers – in fact, 3.09 per cent. They argued that this departure from normality, constituting a 'hump' at the lower end of the curve, was due to the presence of children with specific reading retardation. Children with specific reading difficulties were not just backward readers at the bottom of a normal distribution of reading skill. Unfortunately, this type of statistical evidence says nothing about the cause of the 'unexpected' under-achievement. The existence of the 'hump' did not imply any biological or pathological entity (such as dyslexia). However, since this question remained of interest to the investigators, they turned to examining the difference between generally backward and specifically retarded readers.

Differences between generally backward and specifically retarded readers

To examine the question of etiology, Rutter and Yule (1975) compared eighty-six children with specific reading retardation with seventy-nine generally backward readers. Of particular interest was whether the World Federation of Neurology's definition of dyslexia could be applied to the specific reading retardates. Some important results emerged from the comparison. Seventy-seven per cent of retarded readers were boys while approximately equal numbers of boys (54 per cent) and girls (46 per cent) were backward readers. The sex ratio of 3.3 males to every female with specific reading retardation is similar to that reported for other developmental language difficulties and suggests a common basis for these difficulties – a possibility which will be considered later on in chapter 6. Turning to 'neurological' signs, there was evidence of definite

8 What is dyslexia?

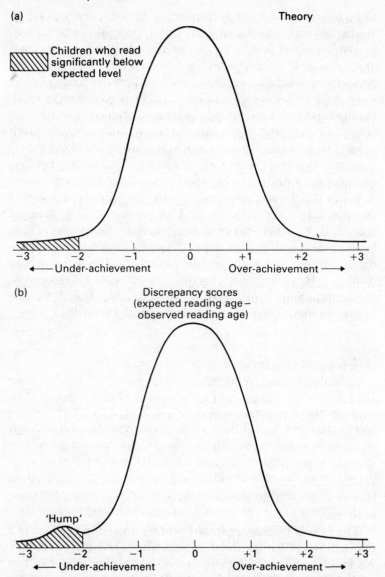

Figure 1.1. *(a) The expected distribution of reading achievement in a normal population; (b) a 'hump' towards the lower end of the curve suggests an excess of under-achievers in the population*

organic disorder in 11 per cent of generally backward readers but it was infrequent among children with specific reading retardation. The two groups also differed in the 'soft' signs they showed. The term 'soft' sign is used rather loosely in the learning disabilities literature: it refers to a symptom or behaviour which might imply minimal brain damage, even though there is no evidence of neurological impairment. Amongst so-called soft signs, abnormalities of movement, such as clumsiness, were approximately twice as common in generally backward readers as in specifics, although both groups had difficulty in discriminating right from left.

Importantly, there was no significant difference between the two groups in terms of speech and language difficulties. Speech delay was three times more common among poor readers (generally backward and specifically retarded) than it was in the general population, and a family history of similar difficulties with speech and reading was reported three times more frequently. The only language measure on which children with specific reading retardation differed from generally backward readers was one of complexity of language usage; in this area the children with specific reading retardation were superior.

So, specific reading retardation was found to be associated primarily with abnormalities of speech and language. The rate of other developmental abnormalities was sometimes above that of a control group but these were less significant than delays in speech and language delay. Finally, the two groups differed in prognosis. Despite an I.Q. advantage, retarded readers made less progress with reading and spelling during a four to five year period than generally backward readers.

The Isle of Wight studies are widely quoted in support of a distinction of educational significance between generally backward readers and children whose reading is out of line with age and intellectual ability However, Rutter and his colleagues have advised against using the terms 'specific reading retardation' and 'dyslexia' synonymously. While it has been claimed that dyslexia is a unitary condition with a definitive symptomatology, specific reading retardation can occur in association with a number of different factors. For example, they argue that there may well be a hereditary basis to reading skill (and therefore poor reading), language difficulties render the child at risk of reading failure; reading difficulties are more common in large families; and the incidence of specific reading retardation has been shown to be twice as high in an inner London borough than on the Isle of Wight. Likewise, serious 'followers' of dyslexia do not wish for the terms 'dyslexia' and 'specific reading retardation' to be used interchangeably. Their reasons, born out of dissatisfaction with the concept of specific reading retardation, are important, and should now be considered.

'Dyslexia' or 'specific reading retardation'?

Perhaps the most valid complaint that advocates of dyslexia have about the term 'specific reading retardation' is its emphasis on reading. No one would dispute that specific reading difficulties are associated with spelling problems, usually greater in proportion than the reading difficulties themselves. Reading tends to improve more quickly than spelling so that 'dyslexics' may learn, through training, to read quite well but be left with low levels of spelling skill. Unfortunately, such individuals are automatically excluded from samples of poor readers and certainly did not feature in the Isle of Wight studies. Obviously this must have a bearing on the conclusions drawn from these samples. It may also influence decisions about educational policy. The spelling of dyslexic children remains their weakest literacy skill and therefore it requires remedial attention. A second problem with the term 'specific reading retardation' is that it is over-inclusive. By definition it covers children whose difficulty has a known cause, for example frequent school absences, and children whose difficulties are due to a lack of motivation or are emotional in origin. The corollary is that these children *will* be included amongst samples of retarded readers, thus clouding our understanding of what dyslexia might be. Moreover, their need will be met by sorts of intervention very different from those appropriate for supposed dyslexic cases. In short, it is really rather difficult to take the results of epidemiological studies which have examined retarded readers defined on the discrepancy principle and to use these to evaluate the concept of dyslexia. We still need to sharpen our definition of what is dyslexia and to what extent (if at all) it differs from specific reading retardation.

Finally, we should take note of some doubts regarding the distribution of over- and under-achievement in reading. Rodgers (1983) was the first to express concern about the conclusions drawn by Yule et al. (1974) based on findings from five populations. His main point was that the reading test which had been used, namely the Neale Analysis of Reading Ability, has a low ceiling of around twelve years which many of the children had attained. In effect, this ceiling reduced the number of over-achievers, thus creating a negative skew: many bright children were prevented from scoring as highly as predicted because they were already gaining full marks on the test. In view of these difficulties, Rodgers attempted a similar analysis using a large national sample of children who had been assessed by individual tests free of floor or ceiling effects.

Altogether Rodgers examined a random sample of 8, 836 children whose I.Q. scores on the British Abiity Scales test were normally distributed. The correlation between reading scores and B.A.S. scores in this population was 0.73 and, taking this into account, the distribution of achievement was determined. On the assumption of a normal distribution, 192 children (2.28 per cent) should have been under-achieving. In actual fact, 194 children (2.29 per cent) fell more than two standard deviations below the mean. Hence the results did not show a 'hump' at the lower end of the curve. Over- and under-achievement were equally distributed in this population.

Similar criticisms have been raised by van der Wissel and Zegers (1985). They ran a computer simulation in which scores were sampled at random from a population of numbers, but any falling above a pre-set maximum were discarded. Hence an artificial ceiling above which scores could not be achieved was created. Doing this showed very clearly the effect which using a test with a ceiling effect has upon the distribution of achievement. The distribution of scores was negatively skewed and there was an excess of low scores in the population. However, van der Wissel and Zegers wished to go further to argue that the distinction between specifically retarded and generally backward readers should be abandoned. Here we can turn previous arguments on their head. Just as the existence of a 'hump' did not imply any biological entity, nor does the absence of a 'hump' refute claims about dyslexia. Van der Wissel and Zegers wish us to believe that the only difference between specifically retarded and backward readers is one of I.Q. But there is hardly any evidence bearing on this claim. Moreover, there is abundant evidence of qualitative differences between children with specific reading difficulties and normal readers of similar levels of reading skill (Frith 1985). In chapter 2 we shall look at some of the evidence.

2
Cognitive deficits in dyslexia

Experimental psychologists have remained neutral about the term 'dyslexia' and controversies within education have not deterred them from investigating children with specific reading difficulties. Most investigators have adopted an operational definition of the disorder. Vellutino (1979), for instance, considers that dyslexia is best studied in children who have average or above average intelligence, intact (or corrected) sensory acuity, no severe neurological damage or other debilitating physical disabilities, and who have not been hampered by serious emotional or social problems, socioeconomic disadvantage or inadequate opportunity for learning. In his own studies, he took referrals of severely impaired readers from teachers and included them if their reading achievement was two or more years below grade placement, provided that they gained an I.Q. of 90 or more on either the Performance or the Verbal scale of the Wechsler Intelligence Scale for Children. In the present chapter, and in the remainder of the book, it will not be possible to adopt a strict definition of dyslexia because we shall be discussing studies which have differed in the sampling criteria they have used. Mostly the studies have focused upon children whose reading and spelling achievement is less good than predicted, given their age and intelligence. Although in principle dyslexia may differ from specific reading retardation, we are not yet in a position to make this distinction.

Broadly the experimental approach to dyslexia has followed two different lines, the most popular being the 'deficit' approach which seeks to identify the cognitive deficits which characterize dyslexics but not normal readers. An alternative approach has been to use a psycholinguistic framework to investigate the nature of the affected reading and spelling processes in dyslexic individuals. This chapter is mainly concerned with identifying the cognitive deficits characteristic of dyslexic children.

Amongst critics of the deficit approach are Morrison and Manis (1982). They have pointed out that it is impossible to decide, given a cognitive deficit, whether it is the cause or the consequence of the reading problem. For instance, if it were found that dyslexic children had difficulty naming pictures, one hypothesis might be that they have difficulty in integrating visual (pictorial) and verbal (name) information and that this difficulty underlies their reading failure. However, an alternative explanation is possible: that dyslexic children have a poorer knowledge of the names which crop up in the picture naming tests because of their limited reading experience. This chicken and egg question besets the area of research into learning difficulties and it is one to which we will return again and again. Linked is the question of control groups. Until the late 1970s, the predominant research strategy was the mental age match in which dyslexics were compared with normal readers of the same age and intelligence. This design brought with it many problems, not least that of I.Q. matching, but the main difficulty was that dyslexics were always, by definition, poorer readers than their controls. Problems were compounded if subjects had been asked to deal with printed materials.

A simple but ingenious experiment carried out by Vellutino and his colleagues highlighted the problem (Vellutino et al. 1973). In this experiment, dyslexic and normal readers aged between ten and thirteen years copied from memory printed words of three, four and five letters following a short exposure. Not surprisingly, the dyslexics were worse at this task than the controls. It would be tempting to infer that they were subject to a visual memory deficit. However, in another part of the experiment the subjects reproduced from memory words printed in Hebrew orthography. Dyslexics performed just as well as normal readers. So it was possible that their difficulty was not one of visual memory at all. Neither group were familiar with Hebrew and, given this, dyslexics could reproduce the words just as well as controls. Their difficulty in the first part was a consequence not a cause of their reading deficit.

An alternative research strategy which avoids some of the problems inherent in the mental age match design is one which matches dyslexics and controls in terms of reading skill prior to the experiment. Typically, dyslexics are compared with children much younger than themselves but who have reached the same level of reading ability as measured by a standardized test. The advantage is that dyslexics can deal with printed material to the same extent as controls because this is the way in which they are selected. So, knowing that dyslexic and normal subjects are equally familiar and proficient with printed words, and that their experience with written language must be approximatly similar, allows a clear-cut interpretation of experimental findings. Essentially, any qualitative differences to emerge between dyslexics and reading age matched controls are likely to be of etiological significance.

The reading age match design has grown in popularity in recent years but even this is not without its pitfalls (Backman et al. 1984). Care has to be taken to ensure that groups are properly matched and that scores achieved on the standardized test used as a matching instrument are not spurious. Ideally, dyslexic and normal subjects should perform at the same level on one of the conditions of the experiment on which they are compared as well as on the reading test itself. A more significant problem is that matching for reading level automatically accords the dyslexics a chronological age advantage. Hence, if the cause of dyslexia turns out to be a specific perceptual or cognitive immaturity which improves spontaneously with age, this is likely to be obscured when dyslexics are compared with reading age controls who are their juniors by a number of years.

No doubt the best experiments will turn out to be those which compare dyslexic readers with both mental age matched normal readers (chronological age controls) and reading age matched children younger than themselves. Few have done so up to the present time. Where possible the present discussion will be restricted to experiments with appropriate control groups and where due attention has been paid to experimental materials. Where this is not possible, the findings of empirical studies will be critically considered before acceptance. We shall begin by examining the theory that 'dyslexia' is the result of a perceptual deficit and move on to look at the more recent theory that dyslexics have verbal processing problems.

Dyslexia as a perceptual deficit

Ever since Orton (1925) wrote about the specific difficulty which dyslexics have with printed symbols and, in particular, reversible letters and words (b/d, p/q, was/saw), there has been interest in the idea that dyslexia results from a visual perceptual problem, A series of experiments carried out by Stanley and his colleagues typifies work in this area. Stanley (1975) investigated the early stages of visual information processing in dyslexic children. Subjects viewed two-part stimuli (usually letters). One half was presented initially and then, at variable intervals, the other half was shown. Subjects reported when they saw one composite stimulus. The results suggested that visual information resided in iconic memory, a store for the short-term retention of visual material, for some 50 per cent longer in dyslexics than in controls. It took longer to pass to the next stage of processing and the authors argued that this could impede the reading process where successive samples of visual information have to be integrated over a period of time.

Unfortunately, many experiments of this type have been discredited because of their use of orthographic materials, and the hypothesis that dyslexics are subject to perceptual problems at an early stage of processing has largely fallen from favour. Instead, a number of theorists, for instance N. Ellis (1981) have proposed that dyslexics have problems when visual stimuli have to be named. Ellis based his claim on evidence from an experiment in which children had to make equivalence judgements about letter pairs.

In Ellis's experiment, subjects were shown pairs of letters which were either physically identical, such as AA, or physically different, such as A B or A a. Subjects had to decide whether items within a pair were the same – that is, whether they had the same identity or were different. All subjects responded more quickly to physically identical pairs (AA, BB) than to pairs which had the same name only (Aa, Bb) .This is a common finding resulting from the fact that judgements can be made quickly on a physical basis. The additional time to respond 'same' to name matches which are not physically identical reflects the time taken to retrieve the letter names from memory. The important finding for our purposes was that, while dyslexics made physical matches as quickly as controls, they took significantly longer than them when the letters matched only in their names. Although we cannot be certain that this difficulty is not just a facet of their reading problem (since a mental age match was adopted), the results do at least rule out the possibility that dyslexics have a basic visual perceptual problem which would preclude letter processing. Rather, their problem seems to emerge when name-coding is required.

Evidence in line with this view is provided by Swanson (1984). Again this experiment utilized the mental age match design but problems of interpretation are not as serious as they would have been had the experimental materials been printed words. In the experiment, Swanson compared the ability of twelve-year-old skilled and disabled readers to draw meaningless angular shapes from memory. During a training phase, subjects traced eight shapes which were arranged in a particular spatial layout. Following tracing, the complete layout was viewed for three minutes and, after a two-minute distractor task, the shapes were drawn from memory. The experiment comprised three conditions. In the first, the shapes were unnamed and the procedure was as above. In the other two conditions the shapes were arbitrarily assigned names (these had to be arbitrary as the shapes were meaningless). Subjects were asked to verbalize the labels, for example dog – cat – bird when they viewed the composite stimulus. The result of most interest for present purposes was that disabled and skilled readers were similar in their ability to reproduce the shapes from memory, but the disabled readers were at a disadvantage when verbal labels were added to the stimuli. Swanson's interpretation was that the disabled readers had difficulty integrating visual and verbal codes. Equally plausible is the hypothesis that they were subject to a name-encoding deficiency. The point would be that when stimuli were given names, these confused the dyslexics but enhanced the performance of the good readers. The evidence is consistent with the idea that dyslexics are subject to a variety of verbally based difficulties, so these will be considered next.

Dyslexia as a verbal coding deficit

Theories linking dyslexia with difficulties in verbal processing (Vellutino 1977) have been enthusiastically supported What is known about the etiology of dyslexia and its association with speech and language difficulties is compatible with a verbal deficit hypothesis and this also makes sense of much of the empirical research. Probably the most consistent findings to have emerged from studies of dyslexic readers are those pointing to deficits in verbal memory and phoneme segmentation processes.

Verbal memory

Studies are virtually unanimous in pointing to the verbal memory difficulties experienced by dyslexic readers. Typically dyslexics score worse than their own average on the memory sections of standardized 'I.Q.' batteries such as the Wechsler Intelligence Scale for Children or the British Ability Scales (Thomson 1982) and there have been many experiments on memory and dyslexia.

A variety of procedures have been used to investigate the functioning of memory subsystems. A popular technique in memory research has been to present subjects with lists of items for recall and to construct serial position curves. These represent graphically the probability of recalling any item within the list, given its ordinal position in the list. Character-istically, items presented at the beginning of the list are remembered well. This is called the *primacy* effect (see figure 2.1). Middle items are remembered rather poorly and recall of items at the end of the list is superior producing the *recency* effect. The primacy effect reflects the retrieval of items from long-term store. These items have been rehearsed and passed into long-term memory. The recency effect reflects the retrieval of items which are still in short-term store and have

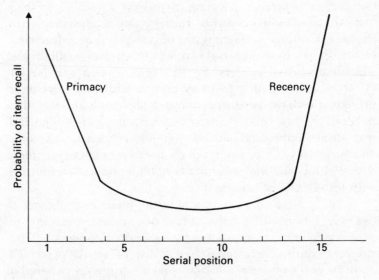

Figure 2.1. *The characteristics of the serial position curve*

not been transferred. If the clinical view of dyslexia is correct, and it is associated with deficits in short-term memory processes, then dyslexics should show a reduced recency effect. But this does not appear to be the case. Instead, a number of studies have reported a reduction in the primacy effect in dyslexic children – a difficulty which reflects problems in retrieval from long-term memory (Spring and Capps 1976, Bauer and Emhert 1984)

At first glance these results are at odds with our hypothesis, but we must bear in mind that items must be 'rehearsed' in order to pass from short- to long-term memory. It is usually assumed that this rehearsal process involves some form of covert speech activity. Now, if dyslexics cannot rapidly access verbal labels they will have difficulty transferring items from short- to long-term store. Interestingly, Bauer and Emhert found that slowing down the rate at which items were presented for recall increased the primacy effect, presumably because it allowed more time for rehearsal. But the improvement was similar for dyslexic and normal readers. It cannot be simply that dyslexics need longer for transferring information for, even given extra time, they were less efficient than mental age matched controls. Rather, this is consistent with the idea that their problem is one of verbal coding. Moreover, in situations where rehearsal is ruled out, dyslexics still do less well than normal readers. For instance, Cohen and Netley (1981) used a running memory task in which subjects were presented with digit sequences of variable length and they had to recall the last three items whenever a list ended. The end was always unpredictable and therefore rehearsal was not a viable strategy. Once again the dyslexics recalled fewer items than controls and the performance of both groups deteriorated with faster rates of presentation.

An alternative way of explaining the memory problems of dyslexic readers emerges from the above and is by reference to memory coding. In an experiment by Byrne and Shea (1979), subjects continuously monitored a list of words presented auditorily. They were asked to make a response whenever they heard a word which had already appeared in the list.

Dyslexic children were as accurate as normal controls at detecting previously received items but an interesting group difference emerged when they mistakenly thought that they had previously heard an item. An analysis of these errors or 'false alarms' revealed that while normal readers tended to think that they had heard before words which *sounded* like words which had actually appeared – for example, they might respond to *fair* when *chair* had been presented, dyslexics made false alarm responses to words with similar *meaning* to those they had heard previously – they might think they had heard *table* when *chair* had actually appeared. These findings suggest that dyslexic and normal readers were using different coding systems to register incoming items: normal readers were encoding their phonological features, dyslexics their semantic features.

While semantic codes are appropriate for use in certain memory tasks, it is generally accepted that if verbal material is to be maintained over a short period of time, it is coded in terms of phonetic features. This view originated from the work of Conrad (1964), who showed that subjects found it more difficult to remember lists of letters when their names rhymed with each other (for example, b, v, p, d, t) than when their names were non-rhyming, (b, x, s, t, w). The effect, known as the phonetic confusability effect, can be seen in young children as well as adults (Hulme et al. 1986). It is therefore striking to find that it is absent amongst dyslexics. Their recall of rhyming lists is as good as that of non-rhyming lists (Liberman and Shankweiler 1979). A similar pattern of results emerges when dyslexic readers and mental age matched controls are compared on tasks requiring the memorization of rhyming and non-rhyming words. While normal readers remember more of the words from non-rhyming lists, dyslexics do not show this advantage. They also remember similar numbers of confusable and non-confusable sentences (Mann et al. 1980). Thus, it has been claimed that dyslexics do not use phonological codes for memory storage. This could well have implications for learning to read.

Recently, however, the findings of phonological coding

deficits in dyslexics have been challenged in two different ways. Hall et al. (1981) pointed out that the data of Liberman and her colleagues does not allow a fair comparison of dyslexic and normal readers. Recall that in these experiments subjects were asked to memorize lists of letters in which the letter names either rhymed or did not rhyme. Hall et al. criticized the experiments because the two groups of subjects perform at different *levels* on the task. Essentially, a 'floor' effect was operating – this means that the performance of dyslexic children was so poor when they were presented with non-rhyming strings that they could not do any worse when rhyming items were presented. When the performance level of good and poor readers was equated by presenting dyslexics with fewer items for recall, both groups were susceptible to the confusability effect.

A similar point emerged from an experiment by Johnston (1982) which made use of the technique employed by Liberman et al. Here dyslexics were compared not only with mental age matched controls but also with younger children who were reading at the same level as the dyslexics – that is with reading age matched controls. When dyslexics were compared with mental age matched controls, the findings of Liberman et al. were replicated – normal readers were subject to the confusability effect while dyslexics were not. But the comparison of dyslexics with reading age matched controls revealed a different pattern of results. Here dyslexics were similar to the younger, normal readers and both showed a phonetic confusability effect.

So, in two experiments where task difficulty was equated, there was no evidence of qualitative differences between dyslexic and normal readers. These findings have important implications. A possibility is that dyslexics are 'delayed' in their acquisition and use of phonological memory codes, and their ability to employ such codes may in essence be tied to learning to read. This hypothesis has been taken up by Olson et al. (1984). In a large-scale study they investigated the performance of 141 disabled and normal reader pairs using the recognition paradigm of Mark et al. (1977). Subjects who ranged in age from seven to sixteen years were presented with a list of twenty eight words for reading. They then completed a recognition test in which the original words were presented together with fourteen rhyming and fourteen non-rhyming distractors. For instance, given the target words *know*, *cry*, the rhyming distractors were *go*, *high*. Given the targets *year*, *life*, the non-rhyming distractors were *best*, *guess*. Each time a word was presented, subjects had to decide whether or not the word had appeared in the original list.

The overall findings were not like those of Mark and his colleagues who had found a larger phonetic effect in normal readers than in dyslexics. Instead, *both* groups made a greater number of errors on rhyming than on non-rhyming foils. However, subsequent analyses of the results according to age revealed a significant age by group interaction (see figure 2.2). The phonetic confusability effect decreased with age for normal readers but actually *increased* for dyslexics. The results produced by Mark et al. were replicated within the age range

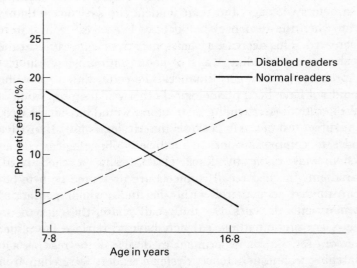

Figure 2.2. *Difference between rhyming and non-rhyming false-positive errors (Phonetic effect) for disabled and normal readers: best fitting regression lines predicted from age (after Olson et al. 1984)*

seven to eight years, there was no significant group difference within the middle age range around twelve years, and a pattern of results, opposite to prediction, emerged in the comparison of sixteen-year-olds. At this age, dyslexics showed a larger phonetic effect than normal readers. These results fit well with those of Johnston (1982) and suggest that there is a change in the extent to which children use phonological codes with age. Disabled readers lag behind normal readers in the acquisition and use of these codes but it cannot be said that they make no use of them at all.

A group difference in the way in which the pattern of performance changed with age also deserves mention. Normal readers made fewer 'false alarm' responses to rhyming distractors with increasing age. It was just as though they were perfecting their use of phonetic codes during development so that ultimately they could use them to distinguish in memory even between phonologically similar items. For dyslexics the picture was different. They did not significantly alter the proportion of false alarm responses to rhyming distractors with age, but their tendency to say 'no' to an old item when the response should have been 'yes' significantly decreased. This decrease in 'false negatives' suggests that the dyslexics were finding ways of coding stimuli and thereby improving memory performance. The codes they were using could not have been phonological otherwise the proportion of false positives (to rhyming distractors) would have increased.

A direct test of the hypothesis that dyslexics use alternative codes to compensate for an inefficient phonological coding system was made by Rack (1985) using a cued recall paradigm. In cued recall, subjects are presented with to-be-remembered items paired with other items which may act as memory-aids or 'cues'. In the recall phase, the cues themselves are presented and subjects have to retrieve the target memory set. Rack's experiment made use of the reading age matching technique. Hence, dyslexic readers were compared with younger controls who had reached the same level of reading which provided a strong test of the hypothesis. In the first part, subjects who were all reading at around the ten-year-old level were presented with pairs of printed words. They had to decide whether or not the items in each pair rhymed. Altogether four different sorts of pair were presented: rhyming pairs which were orthographically similar, e.g. farm – harm, rhyming pairs which were orthographically dissimilar, e.g. rose – goes, non-rhyming pairs which were orthographically similar, e.g. low – how and non-rhyming pairs which were orthographically dissimilar, e.g. stood – car. In the second part of the experiment, the children were unexpectedly presented with a cue-word from each pair (such as *harm*) and they were asked to recall the word with which it had previously been presented – in this case *farm*. The effectiveness of the various types of cue – rhyming or non-rhyming, orthographically similar or dissimilar, allowed an assessment of the type of coding used by the children.

Importantly, the overall performance of the two groups was quantitatively similar. However, success was attained in different ways by dyslexic and normal readers. Normal readers recalled best the words which had been paired with rhyming partners, for example, head – said, regardless of orthographic similarity. In contrast, the dyslexics recalled best the pairs which were orthographically similar, for example, harm – warm, regardless of rhyming similarity.

Rack's results suggest that dyslexic readers were coding items differently from normal readers. They used the visual or orthographic features of words as a basis for recall whereas normal readers used phonetic or phonological codes. The difference was not due to the fact that the subjects had been presented with the original pairs through the visual modality because, when stimuli were presented through the auditory modality, the dyslexics again recalled a greater number of the pairs which had been paired with orthographically similar partners. The results are important because they show that, although dyslexic children do not make as much use of a phonetic code in memory as normal readers, they do have alternative codes available. They can use these in certain circumstances to compensate for their deficiency. Therefore, when compared with younger reading age matched controls, they may score at a similar level on memory tests. Dyslexics have a *specific* memory deficit; because they have other resources available they do not suffer a *generalised* learning difficulty.

The idea that dyslexics use different coding systems from those of normal readers fits more easily into a level of processing framework for memory (Craik and Lockhart 1972) than into a model which separates short- and long-term memory systems (Atkinson and Shiffrin 1968). The central feature of this approach is that the probability of memorizing an item is determined by the way in which the item was processed at input. In general, the more elaborate the memory trace formed for an item, the better it will be remembered. Some people find it easier to remember a list of words if they imagine pictures to link with the words. After all, it makes sense that the more codes there are associated with an item in memory, the greater the number of cues the subject will have available for accessing and recalling that item. If dyslexic children are not able to use phonological memory codes with ease, the probability of their recalling a memory item will be reduced accordingly. Moreover, their performance will be affected most markedly in situations where the use of phonetic codes is obligatory. As we shall see, the tasks of learning to read and learning to spell draw heavily upon phonetic memory codes. Therefore, the dyslexic child is at a great disadvantage in these settings. Another reason why dyslexic children have problems with reading and spelling is that in an alphabetic script such as English these processes require phoneme segmentation skill. We turn now to aspects of auditory processing, including segmentation ability, to see how dyslexics fare.

Segmentation and speech perception

From around four years of age, children begin to be able to divide the sound stream up into syllables so that, for example, they can split the word 'buttercup' into three units, namely 'but', 'er', 'cup'. The ability to divide words into single speech segments, called phoneme segmentation, does not emerge until later at around five or six. When children can divide words at the level of the phoneme – for instance, when they can split 'but' into the components 'b', 'u', 't' – they are said to have 'phoneme awareness' and this is thought to be an important pre-reading skill (Liberman et al. 1977). The work of Bradley and Bryant (1983) amongst others suggests that early segmentation skill predicts later reading achievement. They showed this in a longitudinal study in which they measured the performance of 400 British school children on tests of rhyme amd alliteration at four years of age. The children were followed for the next four years and when they were eight their reading and spelling abilities were tested. Children who had done well on the segmentation tests at four turned out better readers and spellers than the children who had found it hard to detect rhyme and alliteration at the earlier age. This was true regardless of the I.Q. or the social class of the children concerned. So we have good reason to believe that there is a relationship between phoneme segmentation, reading and spelling skill. It could be that segmentation ability structures word perception – at the very least, the ability to analyse the sound stream is necessary if childen are to understand the alphabetic relationship between graphemes and phonemes (Rozin and Gleitman 1977). Without phoneme awareness the child can learn a pronunciation for the printed word BAT, but this will not allow him or her to read subsequent words containing the same letters, such as TAB. In order to appreciate the correspondence between the letters and the sounds in printed words, the child needs to be able to segment phonemically.

On the other hand, Morais and his colleagues have argued that phonemic awareness is a consequence not a cause of learning to read (Morais et al. 1979). While working with adult literacy students in Portugal, they administered an 'elision' task in which subjects were presented with pairs of words differing by the addition of a single phoneme, for example, 'slit' – 'sit'. The task was to say how one member of the pair (slit) could be changed to give the other (sit). In this instance the correct response would be by removing the 'l'. The findings were striking. Students could not complete this task prior to enrolment in the literacy programme but, after learning to read, they carried out the task successfully.

Thus, there is some dispute as to whether phonemic awareness is a cause or a consequence of learning to read. The argument seems to hinge around definitions of phoneme awareness and segmentation skill, which are not interchangeable. Children as young as three years of age appreciate and may even generate their own rhymes. Therefore they must be aware of the sound properties of words. To the extent that they are, they possess some segmentation skill, but obviously their ability to make phonemic distinctions improves with age. Furthermore, to appreciate phonemic structure implicitly is a far cry from being able to reflect explicitly upon it and it could be that the acquisition of literacy exploits the child's natural awareness of sounds, but reading and spelling, in their turn, enhance the child's conscious awareness of phonemic segments. It is this change in the child's concept of the phonemes in words which probably accounts for improvements in performance on artificial segmentation tasks such as 'elision' and was picked up in the studies of Morais and his colleagues (Snowling and Perin 1983).

The literature on phoneme segmentation in both normally developing and dyslexic readers is extremely varied. Tasks which have been used to examine segmentation skill include tapping out the individual sounds in syllables, for example 'b', 'a', 't'; adding or subtracting phonemes, for example adding 's' to 'lip' to give 'slip'; detecting rhyming relationships between words; blending, that is synthesizing words from phonemes, like 'slip' from 's' + 'l' + 'i' + 'p'; and generating spoonerisms, for instance, swapping the initial sounds of 'John Lennon' to give 'Lon Jennon' (Perin 1983). Disabled readers do significantly less well than their age-matched peers on these tests. More importantly, even though these tests are auditory, dyslexics actually do less well than reading age matched controls who are younger than themselves. Bradley and Bryant (1978) found that disabled readers who were twelve years of age but reading at the eight year level did less well than normal eight-year-olds on the task they had used to 'screen' four- and five-year-olds in their longitudinal study. In this task, they presented the children with four words auditorily – for instance 'cat, hat, *net*, fat'. Subjects had to decide which was the odd one out. This could be either the one which did not rhyme – as in the example – or the one which did not start with the same sound as the others, for example, 'sun, see, sock, *rag*'. The disabled readers made more errors on these sound categorization tasks in spite of a chronological age advantage. They also brought to mind fewer appropriate items on a second task in which they had to generate rhyming words.

Interestingly, segmentation problems often coincide with verbal memory problems. However, since the ease with which segmentation tasks can be understood, the memory demands they impose and the types of response they require all vary, a child could fail for any one of a number of reasons. In principle, a poor score could be achieved because of difficulties at the level of speech perception (sometimes called input phonology), speech production (output phonology) or phonological memory.

A few studies have considered the possibility that dyslexic children have difficulties at the level of speech perception. Brandt and Rosen (1980) investigated the perception of stop consonants such as [da] and [ga] by dyslexic and normal readers. Dyslexic children appeared to be extracting and encoding phonemic information like children at a younger developmental level. In a more extensive study, Godfrey et al. (1981) found significant differences between dyslexics and controls aged ten years in both identification and discrimination tasks. Although dyslexics were not markedly impaired, they were inconsistent in their phonetic classification of auditory cues. Before interpreting these findings it is worth considering for a moment how these tasks were carried out. For the purposes of discrimination, subjects were asked to respond 'same' or 'different' to two auditorily presented items.

In tests of phoneme identification, they had to decide whether the phoneme they had heard was one or other of two prescribed phonemes, for instance [ba] or [ga]. In both cases there were a finite number of responses yet, even given this redundancy, the dyslexics were inconsistent. It goes without saying that in a less structured situation they might be at a greater disadvantage. Just such a situation could arise in learning to read when a child is told that the letter 'c' says 'k' but mistakenly believes that the teacher is saying 'g'.

Brady et al. (1983) have suggested that the verbal memory difficulties of disabled readers may stem from equally subtle problems with speech perception. In an important experiment they showed that eight-year-old poor readers made more errors than good readers of the same age when repeating single-syllable words presented with noise masking. In this procedure, words were recorded on to tape for auditory presentation but background noise was added to the signal, making it more difficult to hear. In contrast, the two groups performed as well as each other when the signal to noise ratio was favourable. So, it looked as though the dyslexics required a higher quality of speech signal in order to perform accurately. Unfortunately, because this experiment made use of a mental age match design, an alternative explanation is possible. In noisy surroundings it could be that good readers make use of internally derived orthographic codes to compensate for the impoverished speech signal they receive. In other words, they might conjure up plausible spellings against which to match incoming auditory information to increase its intelligibility. Since the dyslexics were poorer readers, this strategy would not have been at their disposal to the same extent.

To throw light upon the nature of the poor readers' difficulty, Brady's experiment was repeated and extended by the present author together with Nata Goulandris, Maria Bowlby and Pete Howell (Snowling et al. 1986b). We tested nineteen dyslexic children aged ten years nine months on average who, like Brady and her colleagues' poor readers, were reading at the eight-year level. We compared them with nineteen normal ten-year-olds (chronological age controls) and, more importantly, with normal eight year olds who were reading at the same level. These were the reading age matched controls.

We slightly modified the experiment carried out by Brady et al. to pinpoint the locus of the dyslexics' difficulty. A hypothetical model of speech processing (figure 2.3) helps to explain this. According to this model, words in the spoken vocabulary are represented within an auditory lexicon or dictionary. This lexicon, responsible for word recogniton, is linked with semantic memory where word meanings are stored. It follows that words processed lexically can both be recognized and understood. In addition there are non-lexical procedures which are used for processing novel or new words, and in tasks such as spelling unfamiliar words (Ellis 1984). These include phoneme segmentation and synthesis or blending routines.

Turning to speech production, there are at least two ways in

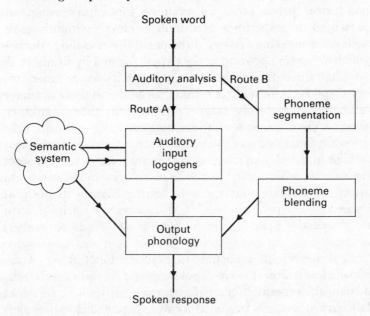

Figure 2.3. *Model of speech processing at single-word level*

which a word can be repeated. Following acoustic analysis, the first process is an automatic one. It involves direct lexical access to the word's phonology and basically to a motor programme for its articulation. This is route A on the figure. The route, via semantic memory, will normally be used for the repetition of familiar words, so their meanings will be accessed at the same time. The second, indirect route does not involve lexical access. This therefore can be used for the repetition of both real and nonsense words. It will be particularly important to children who are still expanding their spoken vocabulary and for foreign language learning. Use of the non-lexical route requires phoneme segmentation, albeit implicitly. Words have to be analysed at the phonemic level before an articulatory motor programme can be compiled. This is shown as route B on figure 2.3.

In principle then, the difficulty which Brady et al. had uncovered amongst poor readers could have resided with acoustic analysis, with output phonology, with lexical or non-lexical procedures. To examine input processing, we presented the experimental stimuli in clear surroundings or with noise masking. To avoid the possibilty of ceiling effects – which did seem apparent in the data presented by Brady et al. – we had three different presentation conditions: no noise, low noise and high noise. Our rationale was that if dyslexics have difficulty at an early stage of processing they should be affected more by noise than normal readers. To throw light upon the functioning of the lexical system, we presented words of high and low frequency of occurrence. In fact, these were the same stimuli as used by Brady, with a few modifications to allow for the fact that we were testing British children. If dyslexics have problems with lexical access or retrieval, then they should respond differently to these words to normal readers.

Next we felt it important to examine functioning of the non-lexical route. It seemed possible that in noisy conditions, or with the repetition of low frequency words, children might fall back upon this route. Moreover, a previous experiment involving the repetition of polysyllabic words and non-words had suggested that dyslexics have difficulty with these procedures (Snowling 1981). So we also asked subjects to repeat nonwords which were compiled from the high frequency items by changing the initial phoneme. Lastly, we did not make a direct test of output phonology but reasoned that if dyslexics had difficulty at this level, then their repetition would be poorer than that of controls throughout the experiment.

Each subject repeated twenty-four high frequency words, such as cake and dog, twenty-four low frequency words, like bale and dust, and twenty-four non-words, for example, gake and tust. One third of the stimuli were presented with a noise mask at the same level as the signal – the high noise condition, one third were presented with a noise mask 3 decibels down on the signal – the low noise condition; and the remaining stimuli were presented without masking. The addition of noise masking made the speech signal less intelligible – rather like listening to a telephone call when there is interference on the line.

Our results differed in a number of ways from those of Brady and her colleagues. We found no evidence of a differential effect of noise masking. The performance of all subjects deteriorated when there was noise and dyslexics did not differ from normal readers in this respect. We therefore concluded that dyslexics have no difficulty with input processing; there had been a ceiling effect in the previous study distorting results. Turning to the effect of word frequency, this was significant for all groups indicating that high frequency words were easier to process than low frequency items. However, while all subjects were at ceiling on the high frequency words, there was a significant group difference in the repetition of low frequency items. Here, dyslexics made more errors than normal readers of the same age as themselves, but a similar number to reading age matched controls.

There are a number of alternative explanations for our findings. Certainly they suggest that, in comparison to their age matched peers, dyslexics have problems at a lexical level –

they may have fewer items represented in the internal
dictionary (Vellutino and Scanlon 1985) or they may have
difficulty in accessing those entries which do exist. But it is
important to bear in mind that with low frequency items they
did as well as reading age matched controls. It could then be
that learning to read has important effects on the developing
lexicon. Perhaps knowing what a word is like in print
increases familiarity with it, making it easier to retrieve. But
this begs the question of why in the first place dyslexics do less
well on this spoken language task than normal readers of the
same age and intelligence. Could it be that the results from the
non-word condition throw light upon the dyslexics' 'immaturity'? Dyslexics made a greater number of errors when
repeating the *non-word* items than both chronological age *and*
reading age matched controls. For them, it was significantly
more difficult to repeat non-words than low frequency real
words – a difficulty which none of the other groups experienced.

The *specific* difficulty with the non-lexical procedures
involved in speech processing boils down to a difficulty with
procedures involving phoneme segmentation and phoneme
synthesis. A direct consequence of this processing deficit
would be to slow the acquisition of new words into the spoken
vocabulary. This could be why dyslexics have difficulty in
repeating low frequency items relative to normal readers of
the same age. While normal readers treated these stimuli as
real words (which of course they were) dyslexics still
processed them as novel items. The reason that dyslexics
could repeat these items as well as younger controls was that
they had a developmental advantage over them. In comparison with the younger children, their lexicon was at least as
well furnished. In fact, an auditory lexical decision test
confirmed this proposal (Snowling et al. 1986; Experiment 2).
Here the same subjects listened to the real words and the
non-words presented in random order. After each item they
indicated whether or not they had heard a 'word' by saying
'yes' or 'no'. The dyslexics did as well as the younger controls
but again less well than normal readers of the same age. They

had knowledge of the phonological forms of fewer words than their mental age predicted.

To recap, the dyslexics' difficulty is not at a sensory level and is not at the stage of output processing. Most probably the difficulty is due to problems with phoneme segmentation and synthesis – a finding which would be consistent which much of the evidence already reviewed. Moreover, when viewed from a developmental perspective, our results go further than to unveil a specific dyslexic deficit. They suggest that, when compared with normal readers of similar age and intelligence, dyslexics have access to the auditory-lexical representation of fewer words. This must place a significant restriction upon the codes they have available for use in a variety of cognitive tasks. In particular, it can be anticipated that they will have great difficulty in accessing and activating phonological memory codes (Perfetti and McCutchen 1982). Additionally, word-naming difficulties might be expected.

The area of verbal-naming has hardly been exploited by experimental psychologists but those studies which have been carried out have revealed dyslexic deficits. Denckla and her associates found that dyslexics were poorer than mental age matched controls on tests of object naming and slower on tests of Rapid Automatized Naming (Denckla and Rudel 1976a, 1976b). On picture naming tasks their errors included circumlocutions (long, drawn-out explanations) similar to those made by dysphasic patients and on rapid-naming tests where they had to give names to the items in matrices consisting of colours, digits or letters, they were as slow as learning-disabled children of lower intelligence. More recently, Katz (1986) reported an experiment in which reading-disabled eight-year-olds were compared with average and good readers of the same age on an object-naming test derived from the Boston Naming Test. The reading-disabled children were less accurate in labelling the objects and had particular difficulty with low frequency and polysyllabic words. Unfortunately, a reading age matched control group was not included. The results are compatible with the hypothesis that dyslexics have difficulty in accessing and retrieving phonological name forms. Moreover, because the words could be defined more accurately than they could be produced, there is a suggestion that they were represented semantically even if their phonological representation was not accessible. However, the conclusions must remain tentative until appropriate comparison groups are tested.

Verbal deficits: an overview

In this last section we have focused upon the verbal problems which dyslexic children have, especially problems with memory and segmentation processes. An interesting possibility is that these two deficits are interlinked – could it be that verbal memory deficits can be accounted for by a difficulty in the application and retrieval of phonological codes, a difficulty traceable to problems with early segmentation processes? Naming problems would be part and parcel of their disability. Unfortunately we cannot answer this tantalizing question at present. To date, most of our evidence comes from group studies and although these suggest that the deficits coincide, at the individual level there may be dissociations.

An important theme running through the more recent work on dyslexia in children is that the nature of their deficit changes with development. While dyslexics have difficulty in the application of phonetic memory codes, their ability to use these does improve with age. In addition, as they progress, they may make use of alternative coding systems to supplement the faulty ones they possess. It is essential therefore that we adopt a developmental framework to help us to understand unexpected reading failure. The least strong interpretation of the findings we have discussed is that dyslexics do not have available phoneme segmentation skills or phonological memory codes at the *right* time – the time, that is, when these are required for learning to read. Chapter 3 looks at the case of a child whose specific learning difficulties were associated with deficits in the areas we have been discussing.

3

Jackie: a clinical picture

Even though there are a number of different theories of dyslexia and even though its very 'existence' has been questioned, the available literature has created for us the picture of a classic 'dyslexic' child. Although not all children with specific learning difficulties can be regarded as 'typical', the girl whom we will discuss, Jackie, was. We shall look in detail at her case and examine her strengths and weaknesses to make concrete our analysis of current thinking.

When I first met Jackie she was eleven years old. It was quite without hesitation that I decided it was appropriate to call her 'dyslexic'. In fact she was quite a 'classic' case except for the fact that she was a girl – and dyslexia is three to four times more common in boys. Jackie was the eldest of two sisters in a family with no history of learning disability. Her birth and early development gave no cause for concern but she was late in reaching her language milestones. When she began to talk, her speech was unclear and she used her own 'words' for an extended length of time. Jackie has always found it difficult to express herself verbally and these difficulties persist now that she is thirteen years old.

Jackie's learning difficulties became apparent on starting school. By the time she was seen for assessment (at ten years ten months) she was at her fifth school and had already received a good deal of remedial help. Progress had been slow and, not surprisingly, Jackie's morale was poor. Nonetheless, a primary emotional problem could be ruled out.

A first and important step was to assess Jackie's general intelligence in order to establish what level of school attainment might be expected of her. On the Wechsler Intelligence Scale for Children – Revised, she gained a Full Scale I.Q. of 115, which places her within the high average range of intelligence. However, there was a significant discrepancy between performance on verbal tests which required spoken responses and performance tests which tapped intelligence by non-verbal means. Jackie's Performance I.Q. was 131, a very superior score. In contrast, her Verbal I.Q. was just 98, a score which fell at the average level for children of her age. The superiority of Performance over Verbal I.Q. has often been commented upon in the literature on developmental dyslexia (Naidoo 1972) and suggests that problems in the acquisition of literacy are frequently associated with an underlying language disability.

On the basis of Jackie's I.Q. score (albeit a minimum estimate of her ability), it was possible to predict statistically (using a regression equation) the level of reading attainment to be expected of her (Yule et al. 1982). At ten years ten months, her expected reading age was eleven years three months (Neale Analysis of Reading Ability) but, when formally tested, Jackie gained scores well below this level. Her observed reading age was eight years six months on the Schonell Graded Word Reading Test, a test of single word reading, and nine years two months on the Neale Analysis, a test of prose reading. Thus, it could be stated unequivocally that Jackie had a specific reading retardation.

Spelling attainment was also poorer than to be expected and measured at the eight-year level on the Schonell Graded Word Spelling Test B. This information alone was sufficient to establish that Jackie had specific educational needs. However, it did not adequately specify what these were. A qualitative assessment of performance was required and three different sources of information were used. First, Jackie's profile on the intelligence test gave some important leads. One of these led to a more comprehensive language assessment (see Klein 1985) and, finally, a detailed assessment of Jackie's written language skill was geared to the identification of both proficient and deficient strategies (Snowling 1985).

W.I.S.C. – R. profile analysis

The majority of clinicians would agree that it is important to be cautious when interpreting I.Q. test profiles. Individual subtest scores are not reliable and therefore differences between them must be large to be statistically significant. Nonetheless, a 'dyslexic' profile has been discussed by a number of authors (Thomson 1984) and, in Jackie's case, this provided valid illustration of her typical style of functioning. Jackie's scores on the various subtests are given below where scores range from 1 to 19 and 10 is average.

Table 3.1 *Jackie's I.Q. test profile*

Verbal tests	Scaled score	Performance tests	Scaled score
Information	10	Picture completion	19
Similarities	11	Picture arrangement	12
Arithmetic	6	Block design	16
Vocabulary	11	Object assembly	15
Comprehension	11	Coding	10
(Digit span)	5		

Two findings are immediately striking. First, Jackie's performances on Picture Completion, Block Design and Object Assembly were exceptional even relative to her *own* average scaled score of 12 points. These tests tap visual perception, spatial and constructional abilities and do not involve sequential thinking. Jackie did less well on the performance tests which required sequential processing, namely Picture Arrangement, a test in which pictures have to be sequenced to tell a story and Coding, a timed paper and pencil task which involves copying an ordered sequence of symbols.

The next striking feature was Jackie's very poor performance on Arithmetic, a test of mental calculation, and Digit Span, a test in which digits have to be recalled in serial order, forwards and backwards. Both of these tests tap auditory-verbal sequential memory, an area in which Jackie had obvious deficits. Her progress in mathematics had been impeded by an inability to hold figures in mind, to consolidate number facts and especially to learn to sequence her tables. Otherwise she was a logical child with a reasonable concept of number.

Jackie's scores on the remaining tests were at the average level but they failed to illustrate how difficult she found it to express herself when intelligence was tested verbally under time pressure. Word finding difficulties and circumlocutions were frequent and Jackie often lost her train of thought whilst trying to expand upon a concept which she evidently had in her head. It was because of these problems that I referred Jackie on to a speech therapist for a more comprehensive assessment of her spoken language ability.

Verbal deficits

As we have seen, experimental psychologists have focused upon a range of verbal deficits which characterize dyslexic readers. Problems in verbal memory, naming and auditory processing are prevalent while visual perceptual processes are generally intact. Jackie showed this pattern of strength and weakness with performance being markedly better when she was able to use visual cues to supplement auditory-verbal information.

Thus, on verbal memory tests, Jackie was able to remember only four-digit sequences presented auditorily and a maximum of five unrelated words. However, she recalled a total of seven pictures presented on cards through the visual modality. Similarly, and in marked contrast to her poor performance on Digit Span, she scored at the 82 centile on the British Ability Scales Immediate Visual Recall Test. During this test, children study a matrix containing twenty small pictures (for example a tractor, some flowers) for two minutes before recall is tested. Jackie was able to memorize this material well with the aid of pictorial cues. Finally, when asked to reproduce meaningless line drawings from memory, Jackie gained a score at the 83 centile (British Ability Scales, Recall of Designs).

An area in which it was not possible for Jackie to circumvent her problems so effectively was word-naming. When administered the Boston Naming Test (Goodglass and Kaplan 1983), she produced several sorts of error. Perceptual errors such as saying 'hippopotamus' for *rhinoceros* were rare. More frequent were non-fluent responses such as 'hor–sea–uh–seahorse' for *seahorse* and most common were circumlocutions. Some of these are given below:

harmonica: use it to blow or make music
pyramid: an Egyptian grave thing
noose: hanging thing, put your head through it
tongs: squeezer thing, to pick up things, clippers

On two occasions the circumlocutions were combined with an unsuccessful attempt at retrieving the target word. When shown the picture of an *escalator*, Jackie said 'exclavator – moving stairs', for *stethoscope* she said 'heart beat thing, telescopic thing, st–stesesemator'. These errors were reminiscent of the phonemic paraphasias sometimes made by aphasic patients. In all cases (with the exception of 'harmonica') Jackie was able to give a good verbal definition of the pictured items indicating semantic knowledge of the words she had been unable to retrieve.

When connected speech was tested, Jackie had additional difficulty. She used gesture to convey meaning whenever it was feasible to do so. Thus, when presented with a picture of a picnic, she gave the following description:

So they set out . . . they went . . . they went . . . I mean
. . . and . . . so they had their picnic, and about an hour
. . . no a few minutes [silence] . . . they . . . they . . .

packed up . . . and . . . got on to their bikes and as they
went down the lane . . . no the hill . . . and their bikes
broke . . . their bicycles broke and so they had to walk
home.

Her speech was halting and punctuated with non-fluent
fillers such as 'uh – um – well – no'. It was certainly less
sophisticated than to be expected given her age and intelligence.

Lastly, a word about auditory processing. Jackie had
noticeable difficulties here, particularly with phoneme segmentation. She confused the following pairs of words when
they were presented auditorily: glad/clad, lock/lot, thin/fin,
and she failed to make the following discriminations at the
single sound level: th/s, f/v, tr/dr, cr/tr, cl/gl. She was also
slow to generate rhyming words and scored at the seven year
level on sound categorization tasks (Bradley 1980).

In short, Jackie was subject to a variety of verbal deficits. It
could be argued that it was these which placed her at a
disadvantage in learning to read and to spell. While we can
assume that Jackie's perceptual skills were good enough to
allow her to cope with the visual demands of the written
language system, her difficulties with auditory skills and
verbal memory would surely have hindered the development
of literacy (Jorm and Share 1983).

Reading and spelling strategies

As we have already seen, Jackie was specifically retarded in
reading. Informal observation of her approach to single words
suggested that she relied heavily upon 'visual' strategies even
though she had been tutored in the use of phonic skills.
Jackie's reading errors included 'crown' for *crowd*, 'angle' for
angel, 'carry' for *canary*, 'imaginative' for *imagine* and 'statue'
for *situated*. Moreover, she did poorly on tests of non-word
reading which directly examined her use of phonological
strategies (Snowling et al. 1986a). Her errors included 'plod'

for *plood*, 'dag' for *diege*, 'shmin' for *shim* , 'dranch' for *drince* and 'sitaponoak' for *stipnoc*. Since she did significantly better when reading words than non-words, she would be best described according to current psycholinguistic terminology as resembling an adult with *phonological dyslexia* (Ellis 1984). This is a point to which we shall return.

So far, our study has centred upon the weaknesses in Jackie's reading. However, when reading prose she had additional resources available and, to an extent, she could use these to compensate for her decoding difficulty. Reading comprehension measured at the ten years eight months level, and Jackie had no difficulty when asked to insert words into 'gaps' in a text in order to complete the story (the cloze procedure). She also performed at ceiling on the SPAR reading test, a test in which synonyms have to be selected as in the examples: An exact copy is a . . . dungeon, doubt, deposit, draughty, dumpling, *duplicate*; and A colonel commands a . . . retina, *regiment*, regatta, religion. Thus, although Jackie had deficient phonological skills, her use of visual and semantic strategies appeared to be intact. Her reading style was compatible with the features of her cognitive functioning which we have already discussed. Where possible she relied on visual cues and, even though it was difficult for her to access the names of target words, the semantic representations for them were available.

Jackie exhibited phonological difficulties in spelling too. While she made a few phonetic errors, such as 'mite' for *might*, 'headaik' for *headache*, the majority were non-phonetic. She spelled *nerve* as 'nev', *join* as 'jone' and *final* as 'fial'. Her problems were even more marked when she was asked to spell words containing three syllables: she spelled *membership* as 'mendership', *umbrella* as 'umderlee', *dinosaur* as 'disonor' and *atmosphere* as 'atmustfer'. Where possible, Jackie called upon her visual memory of word-spellings. For instance, her first attempt at *brought* was 'bourgth', she spelled *island* as 'isand', *pair* as 'piar' and *police* as 'plieoce'. Unfortunately this strategy was ineffective because spelling, by its nature a sequential process, is closely tied to auditory and phonological skill

(Frith and Frith 1980). In spelling, auditory information has to be transcribed. Individual sounds must be segmented from words and their sequential order maintained during the transcription process. Neither Jackie's segmentation nor her auditory sequencing skills were good Hence, her spelling suffered.

Finally, a word about Jackie's essay-writing skills. Creative writing poses the greatest of hurdles, requiring as it does the free flow of ideas, the appropriate choice of words, the use of a variety of sentence structures, and all with due attention to spelling, handwriting and punctuation. It was only with handwriting that Jackie had no difficulty. Recall the trouble she had in describing the picnic story (p. 41). It therefore will come as no surprise that she had difficulty committing this story to paper. In eight minutes she produced the following written description:

> A family went on a trip on their bick biyes, to watch the cows being mo milked and also to have a Picknick. So their they set out.

This account of Jackie gives a clear image of a 'typical' dyslexic child. But more importantly, her case illustrates that 'dyslexia' means more than just failure to read. Chapters 1 and 2 considered the etiology of dyslexia and its associated cognitive deficits. In later chapters we shall review recent work which analyses the reading and spelling processes of dyslexic children. To arrive at a theoretical understanding of this developmental disorder, and particularly how it changes with time, it is vital to consider these different perspectives rather than focus on one to the exclusion of others. Furthermore, if we are to understand why children like Jackie fail to acquire literacy skills in the usual way, we must first discuss the development of reading and spelling in normal children. It is to this task we now turn.

4

The development of written language skills

Long before children start to read, they master the use of spoken words. Hence, they come to reading with a well-formed system for the recognition, understanding and production of spoken language as depicted in figure 2.3. The primary goal of reading acquisition is to integrate a system for processing written language with the one which already exists for the processing of spoken words (La Berge and Samuels 1974).

A child's first encounter with printed words is in his or her immediate environment. Children may learn to recognize their own names, the name of their street, or the name on the cereal packet they see every morning. They probably will not recognize these words outside their usual context, but nevertheless this knowledge constitutes an early stage in the development of reading skill. At about the same time, children can be seen to turn the pages of a book, sometimes confidently 'reading' aloud guided by the pictures. Their primitive reading attempts are important because they help establish the concept of what reading is, that is the extraction of meaning from the printed page – and they lay the foundation for the 'linguistic guessing' which Marsh et al. (1981) consider to be the first stage of reading proper.

A common misconception is that children read by sounding out words. In fact, most theorists believe that early reading is visually based with children establishing the association

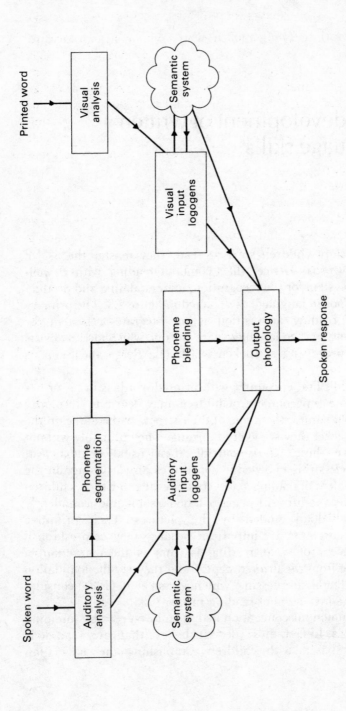

Figure 4.1. Model of the 'logographic' reading system

between printed and spoken words via a straightforward visual-verbal process of paired associate learning. Frith (1985) proposes that children use the same perceptual and memory skills in their first reading attempts as they do to memorize other visual events in their environment. Words are remembered according to minimal visual features. A striking example is provided by the boy who knew *television* because it had two dots – above the *i*'s (Morag Stuart, personal communication).

Moreover, children's errors at this early stage throw light upon the way in which the first reading vocabulary is organized in memory. Seymour and Elder (1986) have studied the mistakes of children during their first year of reading instruction. Reading errors came predominantly from the set of words which had already been taught to the children and there was a tendency for them to produce misreadings similar in length to target items. One child read *policeman* as 'children', saying: 'I know it's that one because it's a long one'. There were also confusions between words with salient features in common. *Smaller* was read as 'yellow' ('because of the two sticks – ll') and *stop* was read as 'lost' owing to the shared consonant cluster.

Several strands of evidence suggest that semantic memory (which houses word meanings) is accessed by young children during reading. For instance, a few reading errors were semantic in nature: *room* was read as 'house' and *big* (mistaken for 'dog' because of the b/d confusion) was read as 'cat'. In addition there were word class effects with verbs proving harder to read than nouns, probably because of their low imageability.

Together these findings indicate that a child's sight vocabulary is stored in a lexicon with links to semantic memory and to output phonology where the pronunciations of spoken words are held (see figure 4.1) Printed words with a lexical representation are recognized automatically although it is common for visually similar words to be misread one for the other and for words of similar meaning to be confused. Frith (1985) describes this early stage of literacy development

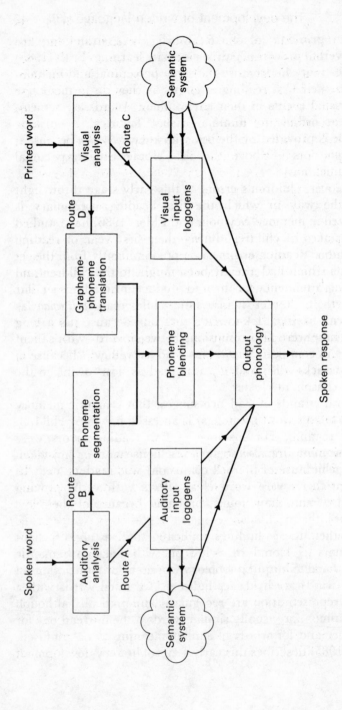

Figure 4.2. *Model of the interface between spoken and written language processing systems*

as the *logographic* phase. Reading is inaccurate and the difficulty of recognizing words increases as more are learned (Gough and Hillinger 1980). Two additional problems encourage the development of new skills. First, because logographic readers have learned the relationships between *particular* written and *particular* spoken words, they can only read familiar words. They do not possess any skills with which to decipher unfamiliar, novel words. Moreover, visual reading is not conducive to spelling (Marsh et al. 1980) and very few spelling attempts are observed at this stage.

Hence, children enter a new phase of development, one where they begin to abstract and use letter-sound relationships, capitalizing upon the alphabetic relationship which is embodied in printed words. Frith terms this second stage in the acquisition of literacy the *alphabetic* phase. It differs from the logographic in that both reading and spelling are possible. Furthermore, the child gradually improves his or her ability to deal with unfamiliar words – these will be read via a grapheme-phoneme translation system (shown as route D on figure 4.2) and spelled by reference to a system of sound to letter correspondence rules.

The alphabetic principle

Transition into the alphabetic phase is no small achievement. Before children can 'crack the code' and understand the relationship between graphemes, that is letter units, and phonemes, units of speech, they require phonemic awareness. However, the mechanisms which bring about advance to the alphabetic phase are poorly understood. Some people believe that the teaching of phonics in school is responsible while others think children extract letter-sound rules for themselves. Frith (1985) has made the interesting suggestion that it is the wish to *write* which brings about the change, since letter-sound relationships are the natural units of spelling. Evidence compatible with this view comes from a study by Bradley and Bryant (1979) which shows that beginning readers use visual strategies for reading but phonological strategies for spelling: hence, there is a discrepancy between the words which seven year olds can read and those which they can spell. The children they studied read correctly words which were visually distinctive such as *school* and *light* whilst failing to read simpler words like *bun* and *sit*. When the children were asked to spell the same words, they tended to spell correctly the words they had failed to read (*bun*, *sit*) and to spell incorrectly the words they had read with ease (*school*, *light*). While retaining a visual approach to reading, these children were using a phonological approach to spelling. It can be argued that they were moving into the alphabetic phase although the transition was not at that point complete. Of interest was the finding that the children could be forced to use the phonological skills at their disposal in reading even though they did not do so spontaneously. Thus, when the phonically regular words which the children had failed to read were embedded in a list containing simple non-words such as *bik* and *dun*, the children read many of them correctly.

One factor which could have accounted for the children's reluctance to use grapheme-phoneme correspondences was a lack of proficiency in decoding skills in general. According to Gough and Hillinger (1980) there are a daunting 577 different letter to sound correspondence rules to learn. Knowing so few of these, the probability of the children failing in their reading attempts was high. It would be natural to steer away from such a task. The probable inaccuracy of their (phonetic) spelling would be less obvious to the children.

Seemingly the improvement in decoding skill is gradual (Perfetti and Hogaboam 1975). Children begin by using sequential left-to-right decoding rules (Marsh et al. 1980). These allow them to read simple non-words such as *dib* and *kip*, but they make mistakes on items such as *kime* and *dibe*. These they would be prone to sound as 'kimmy' and 'dibby'. Only at a later stage do they use hierarchical decoding rules enabling pronunciation of items of this type. Even later still, children begin to use higher-order correspondences such as the soft 'g' rule. This rule states that 'g' followed by e, i, or y sounds like 'j'. When children have mastered this rule (and others of the same ilk), *gime* will be pronounced 'jime', *hage* as 'haije'. This level of performance may only be achieved at college level.

The development of spelling

The changes in a child's spelling proficiency are an important aspect of literacy development. Children's early scribblings suggest that they know how print should look before they know any letters. These may serve to establish the concept that writing is the transcription of verbal messages. As soon as children learn letter names, they use this knowledge to construct simple words. 'GNYS' for *genius* (Bissex 1980) and 'EFNCH' for *adventure* are good examples. At first, children might only write one letter corresponding to a salient sound in the words they attempt. For example, they might write 's' for *dress*, 'l' for *elevator*. Later, boundary sounds are used but medial sounds still ignored – 'BK' corresponds to *back*, 'MP' to *map* (Ehri 1985).

The small amount of spelling which can be accomplished during the logographic phase is of a 'telegraphic' nature, and even when children enter the alphabetic phase they have difficulty with the phonetic sequences of words. Ehri (1985) refers to the *semi-phonetic* stage of spelling when consonant clusters are overlooked, as in the spellings of 'FEZ' for *friends*, 'HEP' for *help* and 'TET' for *tent* (Read 1971). Another characteristic is that consonant voicing errors occur, for example 'PLOUSIS' might be written for *blouses*, 'BOBE' for *bumpy* and 'TREF' for *twelve*.

It is likely that aspects of the child's phoneme awareness and segmentation skill account for the rule-governed spelling mistakes they make during the semi-phonetic stage. Work relating to this issue has been carried out by Rebecca Treiman. Her experiments were motivated by the theory that syllables consist of two sub-units: an *onset*, that is an initial consonant or consonant cluster, and a *rime*, that is a vowel and any following consonants. The onset of the spoken syllable 'stop' is 'st', the rime is 'op'. Treiman (1985a) found that eight-year-olds learned spoken word games requiring that onsets and rimes be treated as units quite easily, although they had more difficulty with games which required syllables to be divided up at different points. To illustrate, take a phoneme substitution task where children learned two separate ways of transforming three-phoneme syllables. In Game A, children heard syllables such as 'feg' and 'jut'. They were taught to substitute the same pair of phonemes, say, 'lu' for the first two phonemes of each syllable. Hence, 'feg' would become 'lug', 'jut' would become 'lut'. In Game B, children were taught to replace the last two phonemes in any syllable they heard with two further phonemes, 'ul'. Thus 'feg' would become 'ful', 'jut' would become 'jul'.

The relative ease of Games A and B depended upon the nature of the syllables the children were given. When stimuli were CVC syllables, as in the above examples, Game B proved to be the easier. This was the task which required the syllables to be split in a natural way – between the onset and the rime. However, when the stimuli were CCV syllables such as 'gwe' and 'fru', Game A was easier. It was more natural to break off the first two phonemes here as they constituted a single unit – the onset. Thus, 'gwe' could more easily be turned into 'sle' than into 'gul'.

Treiman's work highlights the fact that segmentation skill is not an 'all or none' phenomenon. We know that the abiity to segment by syllable precedes the ability to segment by phoneme. Treiman's findings suggest that there is at least one intermediate level at which the child can divide syllables into onsets and rimes but still cannot analyse subsyllabic units. At this stage, consonant clusters are treated as single units and this affects the child's ability to read these units and especially to spell them (Treiman 1985b). Linguistic considerations may also account for the particular way in which clusters are simplified in spelling. Tony Marcel, working with adults (Marcel 1980a), and the present author working with children (Snowling 1982), showed that nasal consonants ('n' or 'm') which follow vowels are quite likely to be omitted from clusters at a certain level of proficiency. Thus, *bump* might be written as 'bup', *candle* as 'cadle'. The tendency to do this is possibly linked with the way in which these 'post-vocalic' nasals are perceived. From a phonetic point of view, it is the vowel which precedes a nasal consonant that is perceived as nasalized. So, for individuals who are not familiar with orthographic conventions, there is some justification for believing that writing the vowel takes care of the nasality and therefore the nasal consonant is not needed. Moreover, it turns out that the tendency to omit the nasal feature is dependent upon whether or not the final consonant is voiced. When it is, as in the example 'bend', the nasal is more likely to be included than when it is unvoiced as in the example of 'bent' (Read 1975). The important point is that the spoken language system and the child's awareness of it, influence the acquisition of literacy. However, it should also be noted that the acquisition of literacy affects the way in which proficient users of the system perceive and process speech (Ehri and Wilce 1980; Seidenberg and Tannenhaus 1979). For instance, although the words *pitch* and *rich* each contain the same number of phonemes, adults think that *pitch* contains an extra 't' sound because of experience with the printed form of the word. Similarly, they take longer to say that *lake* rhymes with *ache* than to say it rhymes with *take* because of the conflicting orthographic information.

Thus, changes in a child's ability to decompose syllables into phonemes makes a significant contribution to his or her spelling development. By the close of the alphabetic phase, children can spell with complete phonetic accuracy and are adept at handling new materials (in both reading and writing). To that extent they will be functionally literate but, in an irregular writing system such as English, being within the alphabetic phase will bring its own problems. In particular, the alphabetic reader/speller will not have any mechanism for dealing with irregular or inconsistent orthographic patterns. *Leaf* and *deaf* would be pronounced as though rhyming, and there would be a tendency to 'regularize' irregular words such as *island* and *yacht*. These might be read as 'izland' and 'y–ach–t'. Moreover, spellings of these targets would be phonetic but illegal – basically *iland* and *yot*. So, for reading of English anyway, there is a final stage of literacy development, one which Frith calls the *orthographic* phase, when reading and spelling are analytic and yet independent of sound.

The orthographic phase

The orthographic reader automatically recognizes spelling units during reading and, by this stage, graphemic clusters such as *-tion*, *-cian*, *-ove* and *-ead* have become totally familiar. Spelling within the orthographic phase is also automatic, with the immediate access to the letter-by-letter structures of a wide range of words which characterizes the fully literate adult. According to Frith, children enter the orthographic phase first for reading and only later for spelling. Transition is brought about by the amalgamation of logographic and alphabetic strategies. In a recent paper (Snowling et al. 1986a) it has been suggested that once children acquire letter-sound rules, they re-examine the words they have already learned to read during the logographic phase. They are then in a position to note how the constituent sounds in these words correspond to the letters they contain, so that they can register their letter-by-letter sequences. Moreover, all the words which they subsequently learn are examined analytically and fully specified lexical representations are set up. These can be thought of as intricate templates. Provided that they are fully detailed, reading will be accurate as responses will only be made when there is an exact match between the words on the page and these internal 'images'.

Furthermore, a fully furnished lexical system affords the reader a new strategy for deciphering unfamiliar words: this is the use of lexical analogies. Marsh et al. (1980) noted that *faugh* can be read either 'faw' by decoding, or 'faff' (American English) by analogy with 'laugh'. In their study it was college students who used analogy strategies. However 'priming' can bias the pronunciation of words long before that time. In an unpublished study, Marcia Williams and I found that children reading at an eight year level pronounced non-words in different ways depending upon the context in which they were presented. Thus, the non-word *yaid* was more likely to be pronounced 'yade' if it was preceded by *maid*; if preceded by *said* the pronunciation 'yed' was likely to be given. Indeed, the state of a reader's lexicon, its size and its current level of activation, is an important determinant of the use of analogy strategies and, by the time the reader reaches the orthographic phase, it is possible for lexical strategies to override the use of grapheme-phoneme translation rules.

In spelling too there is a shift from exclusive reliance on letter–sound relationships to the use of word-based spelling patterns. According to Ehri (1985), the phonetic stage of spelling is followed by a *morphemic* stage in which regularities characterizing a number of word spellings, e.g. silent 'e', and subunits which carry meaning, e.g. -tion, -ing, de-, are brought to bear when generating spellings. The acquisition of the body of knowledge required to perfect this strategy continues for several years and is still incomplete in a fair proportion of literate adults. Although it is sometimes said that reading and spelling are independent processes, it is clear that exposure to printed words (through reading) is vital if this final phase of proficient spelling is to be reached.

Theories of literacy development

We have looked at ideas about literacy develoment emanating from the theories of Marsh and Desberg (1983), Frith (1985) and Ehri (1985) (see table 4.1). Following a stage of pre-reading and pre-writing, the child enters a phase which Frith calls the logographic and Marsh refers to as discrimination – net learning. At this point spelling is rudimentary although, to use Ehri's terminology, some semi-phonetic skills may be developing. Phonemic awareness allows entry to the

Table 4.1 Theories of literacy development: stages in the development of orthographic knowledge as viewed by Marsh and Desberg (1983), Frith (1985) and Ehri (1985). (Time moves vertically down through figure.)

Marsh		Frith		Ehri	
Reading	Spelling	Reading	Spelling	Reading	Spelling
(1) Linguistic guessing		Logographic phase (1)		Increasing knowledge of word-specific spellings	
(2) Discrimination net-learning	(1) Sequential encoding		Alphabetic phase (1)	Shared body of knowledge — ← Letter knowledge → — ← Semiphonetic strategies →	
(3) Sequential decoding		Alphabetic phase (2)		← Phonetic strategies →	
(4) Hierarchical decoding	(2) Hierarchical encoding	Orthographic phase (1)	Orthographic phase (2)	← Morphemic strategies →	
(5) Morphophonemic analogy	(3) Analogies			Gradual increase in 'sight vocabulary' which is organized into orthographic neighbourhoods	

alphabetic phase which subsumes Marsh's sequential and hierarchical decoding stages and accommodates Ehri's phonetic spelling stage. Finally, Frith's orthographic phase seems to correspond to the time when Marsh considers analogy strategies emerge for reading and Ehri speaks of morphemic spelling.

A number of qualifications need to be made about the above framework if the development of literacy is to be fully understood. It is crucial to understand that being in any one phase of development does not imply that knowledge characteristic of a more advanced stage is unavailable or that earlier strategies cannot be applied. In an experiment carried out a few years ago it was shown that beginning readers could recognize more than just features of words they knew (Snowling and Frith 1981). In this experiment, seven-year-olds were presented with stories which retained either sound, shape or orthographic cues. In the sound-cue condition, the words were written phonetically, for example *white* was written as *wite*. Consequently word shape cues were removed and orthographic cues were distorted. In the shape-cue condition, word shape was retained so that words like *rabbit* were written as *raddif* but orthographic cues were destroyed and the words could not be read phonically. Finally, in the orthographic cue condition, each letter was written in a different typeface. This manipulation destroyed word shape information but the possibility of reading the words by sound was retained as in the normal text. Examples of the experimental materials are shown in figure 4.3.

To our surprise, subjects did best when orthographic cues were retained even though these texts had quite a bizarre appearance. They did less well when they had to rely upon word sound cues as in the condition when the texts were written phonetically, and when they had to go on word shape alone in the shape cue condition. Although the children were relative novices when it came to reading, they exhibited some of the characteristics of the orthographic phase in this context. Reading was based on neither shape nor sound cues alone. They must have already extrapolated the letter-by-letter

Mothur gaiv Tom a redd bocks.
Tom tuk it to hiz desc. Hee

lookcd in tho bcx fcr hjs tcys.
Thcn ouf camc a blaek blrd.

Ro3ln HoppPed up to MY wiNdOw.
I gAVE hER SOME bREaD. SHE mAdE

Figure 4.3. *Experimental materials used by Snowling and Frith (1981)*

orthographic information pertaining (at least) to the words they knew.

Similarly, Ehri has argued that young spellers can have available the detailed information which they require to spell a reasonable number of words in their repertoire without necessarily being morphemic spellers. Accordingly, she proposed that children build up knowledge of specific word spellings alongside the three stages in the development of orthographic knowledge. Spellings stored in memory may be more advanced structurally than the spellings which can be generated for unfamiliar words.

In short, children can simultaneously possess knowledge at one level of development and habitually use strategies more characteristic of another stage. Furthermore, different bodies of orthographic knowledge and different reading and spelling strategies will interact during the acquisition process. We have already mentioned how alphabetic spelling strategies are required for laying down the fully specified lexical representations used within the orthographic phase. Alphabetic strategies continue to have a further function which is to allow the individual to generate possible phonetic spellings. But after having done so, it is advantageous if the speller can refer back to lexical representations to check the orthographic accuracy of his or her spelling attempts. Thus, a body of knowledge *created* by the application of one strategy is used to *check* the product of that same strategy's use in another situation. It follows that if an individual has a problem with any one stage of literacy development there will be a consequent effect upon other parts of the process.

Individual differences

The theories of literacy development which we have considered propose an ordered sequence of stages or phases. However, the possibility remains that children will differ in the path they take to achieve proficiency. Baron and Treiman have investigated differences in the strategies children adopt for reading and spelling (Baron and Treiman 1980; Baron et al. 1980). They found two types of reader in the normal child population. They described these as 'Chinese' readers if they read holistically, after the fashion of the Chinese, or as 'Phoenicians' if they made use of the alphabetic links between letters and sounds as the originators of the alphabet did. Thus, 'Chinese' readers found exception words such as *come* easier to read than non-words such as *gome* and, by contrast, 'Phoenician' readers found non-words such as *tays* relatively easier than exception words like *says*. The Chinese-Phoenician dimension can be extended to spelling and individual differences tend to be consistent across tasks (Treiman 1984b).

'Chinese' subjects make considerable use of word-specific associations when reading and spelling. Commonly their reading might be described as 'visual'. They also make meaning preserving errors (e.g. reading *plausible* as 'possible', suggesting that they directly access the semantic memory system at word recognition. Conversely, 'Phoenicians' rely heavily upon spelling-sound rules. It could be said that they use a sound-based approach and this is supported by the fact that they make sound-preserving errors, like reading *broad* as 'brode'. Thus, 'Chinese' readers exhibit features characteristic of both the logographic and the orthographic phases. 'Phoenicians' are more like readers within the alphabetic phase. However, since these individual differences are evident even in proficient adult readers (Baron and Strawson 1976), they cannot be understood purely as different stages of development.

An alternative worthy of consideration is that individual differences are preferences or styles of processing which originate early in development and are reinforced but which do not impede the acquisition of literacy skills. Take the 'Chinese' reader. It turns out that these individuals do less well on sound categorization tasks than 'Phoenicians'. It is conceivable that, although entry to the alphabetic phase has come about normally, these readers were so much more efficient with a visual approach that it was retained and the use of alphabetic skills never perfected. Perhaps letter-sound rules are only used when it is obligatory to do so – for example to register the letter-by-letter structures of words for spelling. This process itself ensures that passage to the orthographic phase is possible. As for the 'Phoenician' reader, he or she may well have started out with an early preference for reading by sound which was retained despite the gradual development of a sight vocabulary.

Hence, just as in other aspects of cognitive development, a series of stages seems predetermined. Individuals with different predispositions, perhaps with different educational experiences, are likely to veer from this set course but the majority will converge upon a similar goal. Only in cases of developmental disorder will there be failure to reach the single determined end-point.

Beyond the single word

Up until this point, our review of literacy development has focused upon the strategies which children use for reading and for spelling at the single word level. This is not the whole story by any means – especially for reading. We must say something about the role which context plays in word recognition, and in particular about the extent to which readers of different levels of ability rely upon knowledge-based resources – that is upon knowledge which exists prior to and independent of the acquisition of literacy.

A popular view amongst educationalists is that reading is a 'psycholinguistic guessing game'. Proponents of this view believe that, when reading in context, children (and adults too) use syntactic and semantic cues to help them to predict forthcoming words. Therefore they believe that decoding is less relevant to reading than more general linguistic resources. A further assumption of the language-based approach is that skilled readers are better at using context in a predictive way than are novices (Goodman 1973).

This view is vehemently opposed by those who consider decoding to be central to reading development (Perfetti and Hogaboam 1975; Gough and Hillinger 1980). The truth probably lies somewhere between the two extremes. It is reasonable to expect children to rely both upon 'knowledge-based' information from the semantic system *and* what is known as 'data-driven' information derived from decoding. This view is crystallized in theories which propose that contextual information *combines* with information made available through the analysis of print to bring about a reading response (Perfetti and Roth 1981) and is a special case of the interaction of bottom-up and top-down processing in perception. It is to these terms that we now briefly turn.

Classically, 'bottom-up processing' refers to the situation where sensory input is analysed initially at the level of perceptual features. In the case of word perception, basic letter features such as ascenders and descenders are detected. Once letters have been identified from their constituents, letter combinations corresponding to sound units can be identified. In turn, these are synthesized and those which match stored templates will be 'received', signalling word perception. In this hypothetical example, perception proceeds from the bottom (the low level featural information) to the top (the high level conceptual information, including word meaning).

Alternatively, perception may proceed 'from the top down'. Here an idea or concept generates perceptual hypotheses which are then checked against perceptual data. For example, the reader might expect the word *table* to be present on the page. This expectancy will reduce the perceptual processing required. All that will be necessary is confirmation or otherwise of the particular hypothesis: for instance, if the word presented began with 't' and had an ascender – b – in the middle, this might be enough to ensure perception. Naturally in more contrived circumstances, say when typographic errors might occur, more detailed perceptual processing would be necessary.

Returning to children's reading, Stanovich (1980) has formalized the idea that top-down information may combine with bottom-up information in an *interactive-compensatory* model of the reading process. The model can also be applied to data from skilled readers. Essentially, Stanovich argues that children use context in a compensatory manner so that when decoding skill is poor, and therefore proceeds slowly, context facilitates processing. When decoding becomes automatic, and therefore proceeds rapidly, context has no effect. In short, children will benefit from contextual constraints between words *not* when they are skilled readers, but when decoding skill is poor. This is quite different from the language-based view.

Top-down and bottom-up processes in children's reading

Evidence for Stanovich's model comes mainly from experiments which have examined the influence of semantically related 'primes' such as *doctor* on the word targets which follow them, for example, *nurse*. Any decrease in the time taken to process the target word *nurse* compared to a control condition in which it is preceded by a neutral context such as *xxxx* is known as the *semantic facilitation effect*.

Posner and Snyder (1975) argued that there are two

components to the semantic facilitation effect. First, there is an automatic process of which subjects are not aware. Activation quickly spreads through the semantic network from an activated entry to others which are semantically associated. Thus, when the word *doctor* is presented, its lexical entry receives activation which, via the semantic system, spreads to entries of closely related words such as *nurse*, *medicine* and so forth. These words are easier to process subsequently because less data analysis is required before a response can be made (Morton 1969). Second, facilitation effects can occur through the operation of a slow-acting mechanism which requires attention. When a prime such as *black* is presented, it is assumed that the reader will intentionally turn attention to that part of semantic memory which contains associates of the prime, such as *white*. If these associates then appear as targets, they will be easier to process. Subjects are in fact 'expecting' them. The corollary of this is that the attentional mechanism produces *inhibition* when material has to be retrieved from 'unattended' locations. So if a target word appears in an incongruous context – for example *table* preceded by *doctor* – it takes longer to read than if it appears in a neutral context (*xxxx – table*).

West and Stanovich (1978) showed both facilitation and inhibition effects in an experiment examining the effect of preceding context on word naming latency. In this experiment, fourth and sixth graders (aged ten and twelve years) and adults were shown target words which were either preceded by a congruous, an incongruous or a neutral context. Words preceded by a congruous context, for example, *the van ran down the HILL* took less time to read than words preceded by a neutral context, for example, *the HILL*. In other words, there was a significant *facilitation* effect. In addition, when words were preceded by an incongruent context, such as *the man ate the HILL*, they took longer to read than the control-words. Thus, there was also *inhibition*. Facilitation and inhibition effects alike were greater for fourth graders than for sixth graders and adults.

Since children both benefit from and are disadvantaged by

context, we must assume that they direct their attention in a conscious way to the contextual links between adjacent words during reading. It follows from the assumptions of Stanovich's model that context will only exert an influence when decoding is slow, allowing deployment of this slow-acting mechanism. Thus, the size of the context effect in children's reading depends not only upon reading skill *per se*, but also upon word familiarity and word difficulty.

Stanovich et al. (1981) examined the effect of preceding sentence contexts on reading of easy and difficult words, both at the beginning and at the end of second grade. Prior to testing, the children (who were around seven years of age) practised reading half the target words. Practice had a significant effect on performance and context influenced the time to read new words more than practised words. More generally, the effect of sentence context decreased with development, but it was greater for difficult than for easily decoded words.

Context can also facilitate reading when the print is rendered difficult to read. This has been done, for example, by covering it with a 'mask' consisting of hatched lines. Simpson et al. (1983) presented nine and twelve year old good and poor readers with words which were either printed clearly or degraded. In addition to this manipulation, the words were preceded either by related or unrelated primes. Poor readers were affected more by degradation than good readers but they also reaped more benefit from the preceding context.

In similar vein, Schwantes (1981) examined the relationship between context and degradation in an experiment comparing nine year olds and adults. In this experiment, subjects named target words preceded either by an eight word sentence context or by an unrelated sentence. The context effect was greater for children than for adults under both clear and degraded presentation conditions. But, interestingly it was found that the context effect for adults in the degraded condition was similar to that for children in the clear condition. Schwantes's finding suggests that the mechanism by which readers combine perceptual information derived from data analysis with knowledge-based information from semantic memory remains the same throughout reading development. What changes is probably the automaticity with which readers can derive or access these sources of information.

In the first part of this chapter changes in decoding skill were examined; the next step is to consider how easily children can access the stored information which is the essence of top-down processing.

How well can children use context?

In spite of the fact that highly associated words such as '*doctor – nurse*', 'black – white' seldom occur together in the real reading situation, experiments examining the semantic context effect have usually made use of these stereotypic pairs (Neely 1977). If we are to hold to the position that unskilled readers benefit from the use of context, we must be able to show that they can focus their attention in a direction other than that to which it would automatically turn (via associative links). We need to know whether they can consciously direct their attention to the part of semantic memory which is likely to benefit them most.

In an attempt to study this issue, a paradigm originally devised by Neely (1977) was used to bring children's attention to the possible relationship between successive stimuli in a reading task (Pring and Snowling 1986). Novel links between stimulus pairs were created by explaining that whenever the children saw a 'signal' they should next expect to see a colour word, for example *green*. For one group of subjects the signal was the word *fruit*, for the others it was *animal*. The children were also told that sometimes they would see a string of crosses: *xxxx*. If they did so the next word could be of any type.

Hence, by using words which were semantically unrelated to targets, it was possible to separate attentional processes from those caused by a process of automatic spreading activation. The automatic process would make semantically related words available but the conscious process could bring to mind the set of words on which the child was instructed to focus. Thus, when the children saw the 'signal', attentional processing could lead to facilitation of colour word items. We also included some target items which were both unrelated to their primes and unexpected in the context of the experiment. If the children were slower in reading these items it would mean they were subject to an 'inhibition' effect – the reverse of facilitation. Examples would be the words *lamp* or *boat* preceded by signal *fruit* which in this case was misleading. Any increase in the time taken to read targets in this condition over that taken in the control condition (*xxxx* – *lamp*) would provide a measure of the inhibition effect (Pring and Snowling 1986, Experiment 1).

Twenty eight-year-old and twenty ten-year-old readers, reading at age-appropriate levels, took part in the experiment. The ten-year-old group responded significantly faster than the younger children overall. However, both groups showed facilitation and inhibition effects. *Expected* targets were read faster than control items and *unexpected* targets took longer to read. Furthermore, fewer skilled readers (eight-year-olds) showed larger context effects than the more skilled ten-year-olds. So, our results provide good evidence that children whose reading age is as low as eight years can direct their attention to specified parts of semantic memory. This is vital if they are to make use of knowledge-based information to facilitate the analysis of printed words and to compensate for inefficient decoding skill. One disadvantage is that the processing of unexpected words will be inhibited. While this certainly was detrimental to performance in this experimental set-up, we would argue that the situation in which context deliberately misleads is unlikely to arise in everyday reading.

If children whose decoding skills are not yet proficient have the capacity to direct their attention to stored information, is it fair to assume that top-down processes will always facilitate data analysis? One possible constraint will be the young child's reduced knowledge of the world and specifically the richness of the semantic memory network. A rich semantic network which is strongly interconnected with the reading system will afford more benefit than a system which does not contain many entries or one which only has weak links with the reading system. By way of illustration, let us consider an experiment in which the same eight and ten year olds were instructed to name the colour of the ink in which printed words were presented. The colours red, blue and green were used for the purposes of clarity (Pring and Snowling, in preparation). The coloured words, for example *girl*, were preceded either by related primes such as *boy*, or by unrelated items such as *toy*. The important point was that the children were focusing their attention on a colour naming task. Hence, any effect of the preceding context was an unconscious one.

The results of the experiment were straightforward. All subjects took longer to name the colour of the ink of words preceded by semantically related primes. One possible interpretation is that the preceding context made the reading responses available early and therefore these interfered with the colour naming responses that were required. The interesting finding was that the interference effect was actually greater for good readers than for poor readers. Quite contrary to prevailing opinion, it was the skilled readers who showed the greater context effect.

The best interpretation of these findings is that the skilled readers who were older and more language proficient, had a richer set of connections between semantic memory – that is the cognitive system – and the lexical system for recognizing printed words than the unskilled readers. Even though skilled readers do not normally need to depend upon context to the same extent as novices, this resource is nonetheless available to them. Moreoever, these strands of evidence suggest that the processes involved may operate more efficiently than they do for younger less skilled readers. Perfetti et al. (1979) reported similar findings from an experiment in which subjects had to predict upcoming words in sentences they read. While poor readers reaped a larger advantage from semantically related prime-target pairs than good readers, they were actually worse at predicting words when explicitly asked to do so.

Hence, as development proceeds the child's ability to decode words increases and, as more words are recognized automatically, the system of interconnections between the lexical system (for reading) and the semantic system is enriched. Even though skilled readers have better access to stored information than less skilled readers do, it is the relative novices who make most use of this resource. An outstanding question remains, however. Can young readers deliberately use context to help them to decipher *unfamiliar* words – words which they have not encountered before? After all, this is a situation in which they will often find themselves when learning to read.

Using context to read 'novel' words

Very few people have tackled the question of how children use context to read novel words. In pursuing this question, Linda Pring and I presented children with a series of prime-target pairs in which the prime was a real word, for example *doctor*, and the target was always a non-word, that is, a novel, unfamiliar letter string. In fact, the non-words were all of a particular kind. They were all pseudohomophones – which means that when read aloud, they sounded like real words. By using non-words of this type, we were able to construct semantically related pairs such as *doctor – nirse* and semantically unrelated pairs such as *doctor – nite*. In addition, we included control pairs, viz *xxx – nite*. We knew that the more advanced readers in our study (who had a reading age of ten years) would be better at reading the non-word targets in the control condition than the less skilled readers (who were chidren of reading age eight years). We were interested to see if in this situation, which maximizes decoding demands, young readers would use context to facilitate performance (Pring and Snowling 1986, Experiment 2). In fact they did. When non-words were preceded by semantically related real words, poor readers read them some 300 milliseconds faster than when they were preceded by a neutral context.

Moreover, they made fewer mistakes. Good readers, whose decoding was more efficient, also benefited from context, but they reaped a significantly smaller advantage – a mere 100 milliseconds.

We were also interested in finding out how the complexity of the novel items themselves would affect performance and indeed, if there was a limit on the extent to which context could facilitate decoding. To examine this question we included pseudohomophonic non-words of two types. The first type were non-words which differed from their real-word targets by just one grapheme or spelling pattern: thus, *nurse* was changed to *nurce* by substituting the spelling pattern *ce* for *se*. These were the '1g' items. The second type differed from the real word equivalents by two graphemes. Thus, nurse was changed into *nirce* by first substituting *ce* for *se* and then substituting *ir* for *ur*. These were the '2g' items.

The rationale for the choice of items was based on that of Taft (1982). Essentially, if novel words are handled by a system of grapheme-phoneme rules, then 1g and 2g items should be of equivalent difficulty. Both can be pronounced (as though real) using a rule-based system. However, if the lexical system is involved in the pronunciation of new words, then the 'visual' similarity of a novel item to other lexical items will be important (Glushko 1979). In short, we would expect 1g items to be pronounced more easily than 2g items. Now, the developing child gradually increases his or her stock of letter-sound rules, but there is also an increase in the lexical system containing word-specific knowledge (Ehri, 1985). Potentially then, both lexical and non-lexical systems may be available for the pronunciation of the targets in this experiment. Which system would be the preferred one?

Our results were in line with a lexical reading hypothesis. Non-words which differed by one grapheme from real words proved easier to read than the 2g items. This was true for skilled and unskilled readers alike. There was also an interaction between context and the 'g' factor. Semantic context facilitated the decoding of 2g items (which were harder) more than the non-words which differed by only one grapheme from real words. The results of our experiment fit well with Stanovich's theory that unskilled readers in particular, make use of context to compensate for their decoding difficulty. Moreover, we were able to show that a child's non-word reading is susceptible to semantic priming. However, contrary to expectation, neither the skilled nor the unskilled subjects showed a significant inhibition effect. The children found it no more difficult to read a non-word preceded by an unrelated prime, for instance, *doctor–pirse* than to read the same non-word preceded by a neutral context.

At first glance, the failure to find an inhibition effect goes against the interpretation that children were intentionally directing their attention to a specific part of semantic memory to facilitate decoding. If they were, there should have been a cost in terms of inhibition of unexpected targets. However, we are not the only investigators to have reported facilitation in the absence of inhibition in children's reading. Schwantes (1985) did so too and we concur with his suggestion that children pool information from a number of sources in their attempt to read. Our proposal was that young readers begin to decode the non-word stimuli using letter-sound rules. The results of this *partial* analysis are then held in some working memory space where *lexical* information, made available via priming of the semantic system, also accrues. These two sources of data, as well as any other knowledge-based information which is relevant, can then be combined to produce a response. The crucial point is that *no irrelevant information enters this process of combination*. Such information is rejected by the system before a final synthesis is made. Hence, unrelated primes have no worse effect than no prime at all.

For the child, then, reading is an integrative process. With development, there are changes in the balance of information which can be, and is, derived from different sources. But essentially, the language-proficient child will bring all of his or her resources to bear when learning to read. To take some examples: when faced with the new word *postage*, children frequently read this as 'post-age'. The more proficient ones will then search through their mind for another word which approximates this attempt auditorily. Many are successful – they can use stored auditory-lexical information to facilitate novel word reading. Stored visual information can also be used to guide reading. Thus, a child may tell you that his response 'garden' cannot be the correct reading of *grab* - because the word is too short. Finally, an example from our study. A child who read *saddle* correctly gave 'horze' as his rendering of *hawse*. However, he was not satisfied with this attempt – referring back to lexical information made available by the semantic links between *saddle* and *horse*, he brought his pronunciation in line with the target item.

The description of children's reading with which we are ending makes clear that several subsystems are at work during word recognition. When reading text, a host of other factors are important (Carr 1985). In single word reading, the normal child will make reference to stored bodies of phonological, semantic and orthographic information to supplement the use of letter-sound rules. Hence, reading problems could, in principle, be attributed to deficiencies in any of these subsystems. In chapter 5 we shall examine the research which has identified deficiencies in the reading and spelling strategies of dyslexic children.

5

Dyslexia as a written language disorder

Having now considered how a normal child acquires literacy skills, it becomes possible to make predictions about why dyslexic children have so much difficulty. In principle the acquisition process could break down from the outset, or within the logographic or alphabetic phases. The point of failure will be determined at least in part by those cognitive characteristics of the individual which set him or her apart from the normal reader. Dyslexic children are subject to a range of cognitive deficits, but for the purposes of reading and spelling it is probably their difficulty with phoneme segmentation and phonological memory which sets them at the greatest disadvantage. As Rozin and Gleitman (1977) have argued, children must realize that spoken words can be segmented into phonemes which map on to the graphemic segments of printed words if reading development is to proceed normally. The chances are that dyslexics will be, at the very least, late in acquiring skills of letter-sound association. At worst, they may fail to do so. Uta Frith has made this hypothesis explicit by stating that, in its classic form, dyslexia represents 'arrest within the logographic phase of development'. Thus, the dyslexic child fails to break through to the alphabetic phase because of a range of phonological deficits (Frith 1985). We turn now to examine the evidence which bears upon her claim.

Psychologists came relatively late to the study of written

language skills in dyslexia. However, some pioneering work was done by Boder (1973), who showed that amongst dyslexic readers it was possible to distinguish between three different styles of reading and spelling performance. Boder's technique was simple. First she presented her dyslexic children with words to read aloud. Assuming that any words read automatically were within the child's sight vocabulary, she then allowed a further fifteen seconds for the child to study the words and she observed their word-attack skills. Lastly they were given a spelling test comprising words which they had been able to read (known words) and words they had not read (unknown words).

Boder described some 67 per cent of her sample as *dysphonetic* dyslexics. These children relied heavily upon the use of a sight vocabulary when reading. In contrast, their phonetic word attack skills were weak. In spelling they managed known words better than unknown words, and their spelling errors were non-phonetic (see table 5.1).

Table 5.1 *Examples of the spelling errors made by dysphonetic dyslexics for words which they can and cannot read*

Known words		Unknown words	
Target	Error	Target	Error
almost	alnost	promise	ponet
awake	awlake	rough	rofot
front	fornt	forge	fogt
laugh	lnonl	tomato	tonto

Source: after Boder 1971, 1973

A much smaller subgroup, some 9 per cent of the sample, showed a contrasting pattern of performance. These were the *dyseidetic* dyslexics. They recognized few words automatically but, nonetheless, had good word-attack skills. In spelling,

Table 5.2   *Examples of the spelling errors made by dyseidetic dyslexics for words which they can and cannot read*

Known words		Unknown words	
Target	*Error*	*Target*	*Error*
and	annd	blue	bllw
mother	muthr	talk	tok
dinner	dinnr	other	uther
work	wrk	ready	redee

Source: after Boder 1973

they did equally well on known and unknown words and their spelling errors were phonetically accurate (see table 5.2). Boder suggested that dyseidetic dyslexics had problems in consolidating 'word-forms' although their phonological skills were normal. She chose the term 'dyseidetic' to distinguish their putative problems in remembering word shapes from those of the dysphonetic group. The remaining 24 per cent of Boder's sample were a group of children who showed features of both the dysphonetic and dyseidetic subtypes. They had reduced sight vocabularies as well as poor word-attack skills, and their spelling of all types of word was poor with a tendency to be nonphonetic. While Boder's early work was illuminating, it had a number of shortcomings. The most significant was a failure to take account of the differing reading levels of her subjects when describing their individual differences. It is just not possible to tell whether the dyseidetics were better readers than the dysphonetics for, within Frith's (1985) framework it is perfectly possible that they had reached the alphabetic phase of development while the dysphonetics were functioning within the logographic phase. Furthermore, it is likely that Boder's mixed group were children at a very early stage of reading development in whom neither visual nor phonological strategies had emerged.

A further criticism relates to the way in which Boder

actually classified her subjects. This was on the basis of the types of error they made. However, Boder presented her subjects with different words, and it is known that different words induce different sorts of error. It is very unlikely, for example, that an irregular but visually distinctive word like 'yacht' could be read via phonic word-analysis. So, subjects given this word would have less chance of displaying their phonic expertise than subjects given a more regular word. In short, the probability of displaying a dysphonetic (or a dyseidetic) pattern of performance was not equally distributed across subjects because they were given different words according to their level of reading ability.

Similar problems relate to the analysis of spelling errors (Perin 1983). Words containing visually memorable patterns (e.g. brought) can sometimes induce non-phonetic errors (e.g. 'broutgh') more readily than would be predicted on *a priori* grounds. Hence, the tendency to make phonetic and non-phonetic errors is not solely a function of an individual's style – it can reflect factors relating to the words with which they are presented. One way around the problems inherent in Boder's study and other similar ones (Mitterer 1982) is to make use of the reading age matched design already discussed. In so doing it is appropriate to present all subjects with the same experimental materials and any dyslexic–normal differences which emerge can be viewed in the light of the reading level attained by the subjects in question.

Reading and dyslexia

A few years ago, I carried out an experiment which investigated the reading behaviour of dyslexic and normal readers and questioned how this changed with level of reading attainment (Snowling 1980). Subjects were selected from a population of children referred to a London hospital where they received specialist teaching. They ranged in reading age from seven to ten years and they were matched with normal readers from a London school according to their score on a standardized test of single word reading (the Schonell Graded Word Reading Test). It follows that the dyslexics were on average three to four years older than their reading age matched controls.

The paradigm chosen was non-word matching. The stimuli were all single syllable non-words containing four letters. The letters corresponded to either three (torp) or four (sint) phonemes. Successive stimuli were presented without a delay either visually (in print) or auditorily (spoken) and subjects had to decide if they were the same or different. If they were different, the difference was subtle and was achieved by transposing the centre two letters of the stimulus (torp–trop, sint–snit).

Altogether there were four experimental conditions. Of central interest were two cross-modal tests: auditory–visual and visual–auditory matching. That is, a spoken non-word had to be compared with a printed one or vice versa. In both instances it was necessary for a subject to decode a non-word in order to complete the task even though a reading response was not required. In addition, there were two within-modality controls: auditory–auditory and visual–visual matching. Suffice it to say that the dyslexics' performance was not significantly different from that of normal readers on these two conditions and therefore we shall not dwell upon them here. However, dyslexics did worse than controls matched with them for real-word reading on the cross modal conditions. When they had to decode letter-strings they had not seen before they were disadvantaged. This finding suggested a dissociation between word and non-word reading in dyslexia. Moreover, there was an important group by reading age interaction, meaning that dyslexics performed differently from normal readers as their reading age increased. This is shown for performance on the visual–auditory matching condition in figure 5.1. As the figure illustrates, performance on the experimental task correlated with reading age for normal readers. This is entirely as expected – increasing reading age brings with it an increase in non-word decoding. However the

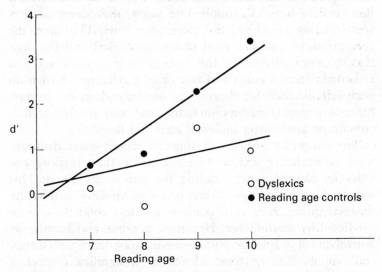

Figure 5.1. *Recognition of visually presented non-words in the auditory modality (d') by dyslexic and normal readers according to reading age (Snowling 1980)*

picture was different for dyslexics whose visual–auditory matching did not change significantly between the reading ages of seven and ten years.

The most straightforward interpretation of these results was that, for dyslexics, an increase in reading age came about primarily because of an increase in sight vocabulary. Unlike normal readers, dyslexics had difficulty applying grapheme-phoneme correspondences to decode unfamiliar words. Their difficulty could have been that they did not know these correspondences – or perhaps they knew them but were slower to apply them than was necessary to succeed in the non-word matching task.

To test which of these two explanations was correct, a second experiment examined non-word reading in more or less skilled dyslexic readers (Snowling 1981). Again the dyslexics were matched by reading age with normally developing readers. The better readers (dyslexic and normal) had reading ages of around nine years, the poorer readers were reading at around the seven year level. This time, the subjects were asked to read non-words aloud and the time they took to pronounce the stimuli in groups of six was recorded. Stimuli contained one or two syllables and within each syllable there were zero, one or two consonant clusters. Stimuli without clusters included *wut* and *tegwop*; stimuli containing one cluster included *blem* and *twamket*.

There were a number of findings of interest. First, dyslexics were both slower and more error prone than reading age matched controls when reading the non-words aloud. This confirmed the findings of the previous study – within the dyslexic group, non-word reading was less good than to be predicted by reading age. However, dyslexics did have some knowledge of grapheme-phoneme correspondence which they could apply if given time. Moreover, a significant effect of reading ability in this study suggested that their ability to use letter-sound skills improved to some extent with reading age even if the improvement had not been detected in a test of rapid non-word matching. Finally, this study extended the previous findings by showing that the phonological structure of the non-words was an important factor influencing performance. Dyslexics did not differ from reading age matched controls when reading single syllable non-words but their deficit was evident with two-syllable stimuli, especially those containing consonant clusters.

The finding that dyslexics have specific difficulty when they are faced with unfamiliar words makes sense because it is in line with the fact that they are slow to learn to read but nonetheless, eventually can do so. Novel words are initially difficult to decode but may finally be learned, perhaps via an alternative route. The finding is a robust one, and has been replicated many times (e.g. Frith and Snowling 1983; Seymour and Porpodas 1980; Baddeley et al. 1982; Russell 1982; Kochnower et al. 1983; Olson et al. 1985). At the level of the single case study too, individuals who have specific difficulties in non-word reading have been identified (Temple

and Marshall 1983; Seymour and MacGregor 1984; Campbell
and Butterworth 1985).

Individual differences amongst dyslexic readers

In recent years it has become popular to carry out detailed
single case studies of children with developmental dyslexia.
These have used the methods of cognitive neuropsychology
and have revealed heterogeneity amongst dyslexic readers. In
particular, two distinct patterns of reading performance have
emerged; in the first, an avoidance of phonological strategies
has been observed like that seen in dysphonetic dyslexia. In
the second, phonological strategies are used and reading is
like that seen in dyseidetic dyslexia.

Children whose reading is of the first type have been called
'developmental phonological dyslexics'. In terms of their
reading and spelling behaviour they resemble adults who,
following brain injury, have lost the ability to read unfamiliar
words. Such patients usually have difficulty with grammatical
endings such as -ing, -ly, -ed, and many have trouble with
function words, e.g. of, for, because. Yet they retain their
ability to read familiar words with understanding and they do
not make semantic errors when reading aloud.

H.M., a seventeen-year-old girl reported by Temple and
Marshall (1983), produced all the characteristics of phonological dyslexia. When tested she was found to be reading at the
ten-year level although her reading, even of familiar words,
was inaccurate. H.M. made visual paralexias – for example
she read *cheery* as 'cherry', *attractive* as 'achieve' – and
derivational errors, for example *appeared* as 'appearance' and
smouldered as 'smouldering'. Importantly, H.M. had significant difficulty with non-word reading and she found regular
word reading no easier then decoding irregular words. Along
similar lines, Seymour and MacGregor (1984) presented L.T.
as an example of a developmental phonological dyslexic.
When studied, L.T. was an eighteen-year-old girl reading at
the eleven-year level. L.T.'s non-word reading was much

slower than word reading and the error rate (some 30 per cent) was substantially higher. Regularity had no significant effect on either reaction time or error rate for high frequency or for low frequency words and, although L.T. could read function words, it took her quite a long time to do so.

The absence of a regularity effect, also noted in group studies by Barron (1980) and Frith and Snowling (1983), and the non-word reading deficits characteristic of these children, suggest that they do not make use of letter-sound rules in their reading attempts. These instances of developmental phonological dyslexia are compatible with the results already discussed from controlled group studies and together they provide support for Frith's theory that dyslexia in children arises because of a failure to break through to the alphabetic phase of development. However, not all dyslexic children display this phonological profile. Children who use phonology in reading (and spell by ear) have been likened to adults with an acquired reading problem called 'surface dyslexia'. Surface dyslexia in adults is characterized by the tendency to read words using letter-sound rules (but see Marcel 1980b). Surface dyslexic patients read regular words such as *fresh, dance* and *treat* more easily then irregular words like *broad, pint* and *great*, and many of their reading errors are 'regularizations'. These occur when irregular words are decoded using phonological rules: for example, *broad* might be read as 'brode', *great* as 'greet'. Additionally, because surface dyslexics read by sound they are prone to confuse the meanings of homophones such as *fair* and *fare, leek* and *leak, meddle* and *medal*, and they can have marked difficulty in understanding what they read. Importantly, unlike phonological dyslexics, one aspect of their reading which is intact is their non-word reading.

Surface dyslexia in children was first described by Holmes (1978) who studied four dyslexic boys who made typically phonic reading errors and regularizations. A more recent case, C.D., described by Coltheart et al. (1983) was a fifteen-year-old girl of average intelligence who was reading at the ten-year level. C.D. was more successful at reading regular than irregular words, she made regularization errors in reading and she confused the meanings of homophones. Her performance was extremely similar to that of the surface dyslexics with problems acquired through brain damage, but her non-word reading was better. (This is a point which the authors do not explain and which does, in fact, create problems for their view. It is more fully discussed on p. 82.)

Seymour and MacGregor (1984) avoid applying the label of surface dyslexia in their work with children but they do recognize a group of children who have an impairment of sight vocabulary extension. These individuals were characterized by serial letter-by-letter processing. This was detectable only in their reaction times to words of differing length and was not obvious as the enunciation of each letter would have been. Seymour and MacGregor referred to their cases as *developmental morphemic dyslexics* and G.S., a thirteen-year-old boy reading at the ten-year level, was a typical example. His single word reading was influenced by regularity. He read regular words better and faster than irregular items and tended to pronounce low frequency irregular words as though regular. Furthermore, he took as long to pronounce low frequency words as to assemble pronunciations for non-words. It seemed unequivocal that G.S. was reading using letter-sound rules and this was borne out by his performance on decision tasks involving printed words. Here, processing time increased in parallel to word length.

At first glance, the existence of a 'surface' or 'morphemic' dyslexic pattern of reading creates difficulty for Frith's formulation. The development of these individuals is *not* arrested within the logographic phase. Rather they have reached the alphabetic phase of acquisition – the problem is that they seem to be 'stuck' within it. However, is this really the case? Sadly lacking from the case studies of children showing 'phonological' reading are data from reading age matched controls. Without these data we do not know for sure whether the pattern of performance they show is atypical given the reading level they have reached. All we know is that it is different from that displayed by (developmental) phonological dyslexics.

With these very points in mind, Bryant and Impey (1986) examined a class of normal ten-year-olds using the psycholinguistic approach found useful in delineating syndromes of acquired dyslexia (Coltheart 1980). The reason they chose ten-year-olds was that this was the level at which both H.M. (Temple and Marshall's phonological dyslexic) and C.D. (Coltheart et al.'s surface dyslexic) were reading. A direct comparison of the performance of these dyslexics with appropriate controls could therefore be made. Their results are important, for they found that the only feature which distinguished H.M. and C.D. from normal readers was their non-word reading. While H.M. failed to show a regularity effect, so did some normal readers, and plenty of the controls showed regularity effects like C.D. This applied to every aspect of reading performance examined. There were always normal readers who performed in the same way as the dyslexic girls. We must conclude that there is nothing inherent in the *reading* performance of H.M. and C.D. which sets them apart from normal readers, so far as *lexical* reading strategies are concerned. Moreover, it was unfortunate that C.D. was presented as an example of a surface dyslexic. The finding that her non-word reading was poor makes her atypical and therefore calls into question her designation to this category.

The question of subtypes

The picture which emerges from our analysis of dyslexia as a written language disorder is that there are (at least) two sorts of children who have specific reading difficulties. Results of group studies suggest that the larger group are children who have specific phonological deficits affecting the acquisition of alphabetic skills. However, there may be another group who achieve alphabetic competence. From what we can tell so far, these children, known as surface or morphemic dyslexics, exhibit the normal range of reading strategies and it seems likely that they perform in a similar way to reading age matched controls. However, it would be premature to draw firm conclusions on the present evidence. Data from appropriate comparison groups is available for only a few of the reading tasks which have been used, and mostly the pattern of performance described is based upon error data. Latencies may tell a very different story. Essentially, a child who misreads non-words as real words may be less different from a child who takes on average ten seconds to read a non-word correctly than their accuracy scores suggest.

Problems of interpretation also apply to studies which have drawn parallels between developmental reading difficulties and other acquired dyslexias. Some of these present too little information. For example, Prior and McCorriston (1984) described a child, N.M., who resembled a letter-by-letter reader. Adults who are letter-by-letter readers have lost their ability to read but retain the ability to spell. So they are forced to 'read' by first pronouncing the individual letters of a word and subsequently recognizing its aural spelling. The time taken to read a word is consequently dependent upon the number of letters it contains. N.M., an eleven-year-old boy, seemed to read in this way. When tested he was reading at the six years eight months level and the only method he had for pronouncing printed words was one in which he spelled out the letters. He used a mixture of letter sounds and letter names. He managed regular words better than irregular, and he could spell relatively well. Unfortunately, though, his reading was so poor that the authors could not fully assess the strategies he was using.

A far greater problem arises when researchers fail to adopt a developmental perspective when analysing their data. Probably the most serious form of acquired dyslexia is deep dyslexia as experienced by certain neurological patients who have suffered brain damage. Reports of children resembling these patients are flawed in this respect. It is worth taking time to examine these reports as they illustrate how an approach stemming from an adult rather than a developmental framework can be misleading. First we must consider the features of deep dyslexia acquired in adulthood. The most striking feature is that patients make semantic errors in single word reading. Thus, they might read *boat* as 'captain', *inch* as 'rule' and *paddock* as 'horses'. Their reading is affected by imageability – words which are concrete in meaning, such as *man, house, tree* are more likely to be read correctly than abstract words such as *hope, love, peace*, and grammatical function words such as *for, when, because* are frequently omitted or substituted for one another. In addition, deep dyslexics cannot read non-words. Taken together these 'symptoms' suggest that several components of the reading system are damaged (Coltheart et al. 1980). There are deficits within both the semantic and phonological reading systems and some patients also have difficulty with the early stages of visual analysis.

Putative cases of deep dyslexia in childhood have been described by Johnston (1983) and Siegal (1985). Johnston's case, C.R., was an eighteen-year-old girl who read only at the six-year level. She was unlike the developmental dyslexics who feature in group studies because her I.Q. was low, measuring at 75 on the Wechsler test (W.I.S.C.-R.) and there was a possibilty that she had sustained brain damage through a blow on the head early in childhood. In single word reading, C.R. was more accurate with words of high than of low imageability. While this is a feature of deep dyslexia we must be cautious because, as Baddeley et al. (1982) have shown, this is also a normal characteristic of children's reading. C.R. had difficulty reading function words and she was virtually unable to read non-words. Out of 382 reading responses, she made five semantic errors. She read *office* as 'occupation', *down* as 'up', *seven* as 'eight', *chair* as 'table' and *table* as 'chair'.

Unfortunately Johnston's data are problematic. Performance levels were extremely low and in the face of such difficulty it is probable that the child was behaving quite erratically. Moreover, the semantic error rate was not greater than chance and, as this is the cardinal feature of deep dyslexia, it makes her diagnosis doubtful. Siegal's work takes us a little further. Although again her subjects had I.Q. scores on the lower side of average, ranging from 76 to 100 with a tendency for Verbal I.Q. to be reduced. All her cases were in the beginning stages of reading, between a six- and a seven-year level. They were unable to read non-words and they made reading errors which Siegal interpreted as semantic. Most common were pronoun (*he/she*) and function word (*of/for*) substitutions. There were also verb substitutions (*walk/run, like/walk*) and some 'contiguous' errors (*eat/fish*). Bearing in mind what beginning readers are like, we cannot rule out the possibility that these were straight guesses where the child made a stab for a word which he or she knew. The only 'true' semantic errors which occurred were reading *wheel* as 'ball' and *gentleman* as 'grandmother'. Even in the case of these errors there is an alternative explanation and that is that the child was reading on the basis of minimal visual cues. The young readers studied by Seymour and Elder (1986) made very similar mistakes.

So, there are problems with the cases presented by both Johnston and Siegal. In neither case were the semantic errors – the principal feature of deep dyslexia – very convincing. Moreover, the reading performance of these children was quite appropriate if we maintain that they were functioning within the early logographic phase of development. It is true that Siegal claimed her cases were quite different from other beginning readers with whom she compared them. However, examination of her data suggests that these were probably not adequate controls – they were all reading at above the 20 centile and this was higher than the level achieved by the dyslexics.

The search for developmental analogues of the acquired dyslexias advocated by Marshall (1984) can direct attention away from the important question of how dyslexia arises in children. There are also serious methodological problems inherent in the comparison (Snowling 1983). If we really are interested in learning why otherwise intelligent children fail to learn to read, we must continue to look for characteristics which distinguish them from their reading age matched controls. This being the case, we need to be critical of the 'developmental deep dyslexics' so far described and of the group termed 'developmental surface dyslexic' (Patterson et al. 1985). These children are certainly developing their reading more slowly than might be expected given their age and I.Q.; they have *specific* reading difficulties but, nonetheless, their development seems to be along normal lines.

Spelling and dyslexia

Far fewer studies have focussed on the spelling of dyslexic children than have been concerned with their reading. This is surprising since spelling is the weaker of the two literacy skills and presents an intractable problem to many individuals. Generally, the studies which have been conducted have been interpreted within a 'two-route' model of the spelling process (Simon and Simon 1973; Frith 1980; A.W. Ellis 1982). One such model will be briefly outlined here – that of A.W. Ellis (1982) – before proceeding to the empirical work. It should, however, be noted that this is a model which describes the spelling strategies available to a fluent adult speller. It should not be applied unreservedly to children's spelling performance. According to Ellis, there are at least two ways in which words can be spelled. If the word is familiar, component letters may be automatically accessed in the *graphemic output logogen system* (Route A, figure 5.2). However, if the word's spelling is not known, a plausible version can be compiled using phonological skills. Starting with speech as input, a phonemic buffer is thought to isolate or segment phonemes which are then passed through a process of phoneme-grapheme translation prior to writing (Route B). This is the route which will be preferred for unfamiliar words and, of course, for spelling non-words. It will naturally figure a great deal in children's spelling when many word spellings are unknown. Thus, it is important to distinguish between direct and indirect routes to spelling production. Since the indirect route utilizes phonological processes, it can be predicted that

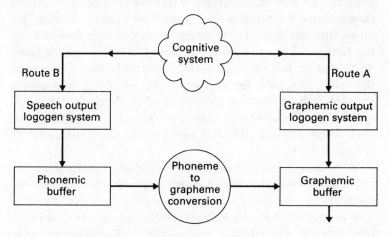

Figure 5.2. *Model of the spelling process (after Ellis 1982)*

dyslexics will have problems with its operation.

Analysis of spelling error patterns has been considered useful in studying the cognitive deficits underlying spelling difficulty and there have been a number of attempts to use errors diagnostically. Boder, it will be recalled, distinguished between dysphonetic and dyseidetic dyslexics according to spelling error pattern (Boder 1973). Unfortunately the procedure of classifying spelling errors is fraught with difficulty. There has been inconsistency in the criteria used for error analysis leading to competing claims in the literature (Nelson 1980). While a number of authors have failed to find differences in spelling performance between good and poor readers (Barron 1980; Holmes and Pepper 1977; Goyen and Martin 1977), others have stressed differences (Sweeney and Rourke 1978).

Recently, Temple (1986) described two dyslexic children, both reading and spelling at similar *levels*, who made qualitatively different spelling mistakes. R.B., a ten-year-old girl spelling at the seven years six months level, made mainly phonetically accurate errors which portrayed the sound sequence of the word correctly but which violated spelling conventions. Examples were 'agektif' for *adjective*, 'rashon' for *ration*, 'fite' for *fight*. These errors suggest that R.B. could use the indirect route to spelling although she did exhibit some 'higher-order failure' of phonological translation as shown by the errors 'discrace' for *disgrace*, 'trote' for *throat*. A consequence of R.B.'s spelling pattern was a regularity effect in spelling – she made fewer errors when spelling regular words than when tackling irregular items of the same frequency of occurrence.

In contrast, A.H., another ten-year-old, spelling at the seven years eight months level, made primarily non-phonetic errors. These included 'childenre' for *children*, 'perss' for *press*, 'cloryer' for *chlorine*. Unlike R.B., A.H. was unable to spell by phonological translation. Consequently he had approximately equal difficulty with regular and irregular words, and extreme difficulty spelling non-words. So, both of these children were poor spellers for their age and their spelling error patterns suggested different patterns of dysfunction. In developmental terms, R.B. had passed into the alphabetic phase, A.H. was experiencing difficulty in attaining alphabetic competence. An outstanding question, however, was whether either of these children were 'atypical' given the level of development at which they were functioning. That is, while it was clear that R.B. and A.H. differed from each other, did they actually differ from normally developing children at the same level of literacy development?

To look into this question, Temple compared the performance of the dyslexic subjects with that of normally developing seven year olds. She found that R.B.'s performance was similar to theirs, except for the fact that she committed reversal errors. On the other hand, A.H. performed well outside of the normal range especially in that he made an excessive number of non-phonetic spelling errors. It is unequivocal that A.H. had a developmental disorder of spelling, and the stumbling block seemed to be the acquisition of alphabetic skills. The evidence relating to R.B. was less clear-cut. While her spelling errors were like those of normal controls, a number of qualifications must be made. First, it is important to take heed of the matching procedure which was a stringent one based on spelling age. In actual fact, both R.B. and A.H. were reading at a level which exceeded this by about one year. On the assumption that reading experience contributes towards spelling knowledge, children *reading* at the same level as the dyslexics would presumably have fewer spelling problems. Since spelling by its nature draws more upon phonology than reading, this in itself is suggestive of a problem in the use of phonology for R.B. as well as for A.H. Moreover, when R.B. was asked to spell orally, her performance deteriorated and a greater number of non-phonetic errors were made. In this situation, for example, she spelled *dancing* as 'dence', *amount* as 'amte'.

Thus, in R.B.'s case, it seems that the use of phonology for spelling was only viable when a written response was required. Writing responses were not timed, so it remains a possibility that the indirect route was used, but only at the expense of time. This might be a way in which the spelling of R.B. actually differed from that of normal readers. We just do not know. The fact is that children's spelling errors shed only partial light on the functioning of direct and indirect routes. Moreover, as children's spelling tends to be tested in one situation only, that of dictation, it is possible that their use of phonology is strategic, especially if they have received phonics teaching. When consciously required to do so, some children may draw upon the indirect route. This says nothing about the usual role of checking and monitoring of this route when attention is not explicitly directed to its functioning. Thomson (1981) reported that, in their spontaneous writing, dyslexics make one spelling error in five, whereas the ratio for normal readers is one in thirty-five. This is a situation then in which dyslexics might make far more serious errors than their reading age matched controls.

So, despite the apparent differences between the spelling errors of R.B. and A.H., there is insufficient evidence to confirm that their underlying difficulty is also different. Rhyming tests administered by Temple indicated that A.H.

had difficulties with sound categorization which R.B. did not share, but these tests were insufficiently detailed to discern whether there was a qualitative or a quantitative difference in performance.

Now, according to Frith (1985), transition to the orthographic phase (the stage which signals fluent spelling), requires the amalgamation of logographic and alphabetic skills. It follows that, at the time when they were studied, this transition was not feasible for either A.H. or R.B. However, it will be recalled that Ehri (1985) suggested that a store of word-specific knowledge could be created alongside the development of literacy skills. In principle. then, a child like A.H., failing to move to the alphabetic phase, could nevertheless gain lexical knowledge of word spellings. R.E., the dyslexic student studied by Campbell and Butterworth (1985), had acquired a considerable spelling repertoire in this way. She was able to read and to spell quantitatively as well as her undergraduate peers yet more than 40 per cent of her spelling errors were non-phonetic. Her ability to distinguish correct spellings from her own non-phonetic errors and from phonologically plausible ones was limited, and she had great difficulty in spelling non-word items.

Thus, R.E. had problems with the indirect route to spelling. In particular, she was unable to generate spellings for unfamiliar words or to run a conclusive phonological check on her written responses. This was why, for example, she was unable to tell which of the following spellings was correct: *terrisetrial, tirrestrial, terrestrial*. In both respects she was worse than her peers who were spelling at a generally similar level. Her development had proceeded much farther than that of A.H. or R.B. yet she remained deficient in the use of alphabetic skills. R.E. was unusual. Most dyslexics fail to learn to spell effectively and do not achieve such a sophisticated level of literacy. Even when they do possess orthographic knowledge it is probable that they take a long time to access it and they may frequently make errors of retrieval. Indeed, Farnham-Diggory and Nelson (1983) carefully recorded the spelling attempts of eleven year-old dyslexics, chronological age and reading age matched controls. In particular they examined the way in which letters and letter clusters were recalled over time. All subjects tended to produce 'chunks' three letters long. However, dyslexics took particularly long to produce a chunk, and were similar in this regard to younger reading age controls. So, in their everyday spelling attempts, dyslexics are not only less accurate than their age-related peers, they are also much slower, even when retrieving familiar word-spellings.

Specific spelling problems

For children who fail to make the transition to the alphabetic phase, serious spelling difficulties ensue. The children discussed so far in this chapter had difficulties with both reading and spelling. However, the term 'dyslexia' has sometimes been applied to children who have spelling difficulties in the absence of reading problems (Jorm 1981). Naidoo (1972), reporting on a sample of some one hundred dyslexic children who attended the ICAA Word Blind Centre in London, noted that a proportion were what she called 'spelling-only retardates'. These children tended to have a Verbal I.Q. score which was larger than Performance. This is usually taken to mean that language skills are better than non-verbal, perceptual abilities.

A similar distinction was made by Nelson and Warrington (1974) between 'reading and spelling' and 'spelling – only' retardates. Children whose difficulty was specific to spelling tended to make phonetic spelling errors. However, children who were retarded in both reading and spelling made phonetic as well as non-phonetic mistakes. The authors assumed that the poor readers' difficulty was linked to an underlying language problem, a hypothesis shared by Rourke (1983), who considered the difficulty to worsen as time proceeds. In dyslexics of this type, it is usually Performance I.Q. which is higher than verbal ability.

The special instance of children who have spelling difficulties in the absence of reading problems has been examined by Frith (1978, 1980) and the work has been extended to adults by Perin (1981). It remains a moot point as to whether these individuals are dyslexics who have learned to read or whether they really have never had reading problems. Nicky, a fourteen-year-old boy whom Frith studied (Frith 1984), had never had any reading difficulty but seemingly others of her subjects were, at the very least, slower to learn to read than expected, given their intelligence. Using experimental methods as well as techniques of error analysis, Frith distinguished between good readers who were also good spellers and good readers who were poor spellers. She called these groups A and B respectively. Group B spellers made primarily phonetic spelling errors. They had particular problems in knowing when it was appropriate to double consonants in spellings and in knowing how to represent schwa vowels such as the 'er' in 'cat*a*pult'. This was in clear contrast to their group A controls who were reading at the same level. The uncertainty of group B spellers was also reflected in forced-choice tests in which they had to select the correct spellings from two plausible versions, for example *successful/succesfull, necessery/necessary*. They also did less well than group A in proof reading tasks and on tests of non-word reading (Frith 1978).

Surprisingly, what first manifested itself as a specific spelling problem could be reinterpreted as a reading difficulty – albeit a subtle one. Frith and Perin (reported in Frith 1984) sought further evidence for this hypothesis in an experiment employing an e-cancellation task. Adolescent subjects were allocated to groups according to reading and spelling skills and they were instructed to cross out every *e* they came across in a connected but meaningless text consisting of phrases. Target words were of two types, containing either important or unimportant *e*'s. Important *e*'s were crucial for word recognition, as in the word *left*, while words containing unimportant *e*'s could easily be identified without actually noticing the *e* (e.g. in the word 'lifted'). It turns out that important *e*'s are found in stressed syllables and are usually at the beginning or in the middle of a word, while unimportant *e*'s usually represent schwa or are silent and occur towards the ends of words. If one is paying attention to detail when reading, all letters, irrespective of their importance in a word, should be noticed, if only fleetingly. The hypothesis tested was that poor spellers do not pay attention to all letters when reading and this has an effect on their spelling skill.

The results of the experiment supported the claim that poor spellers do not read for 'detail'. While good and poor spellers were equally able to cancel important *e*'s, poor spellers missed significantly more unimportant *e*'s. Thus, poor spellers attend mostly to the more 'salient' letters which occur earlier in the word or have an explicit relationship to pronunciation. This has important consequences for their spelling, and mistakes will tend to cluster on the 'unimportant' parts of words. Unfortunately educators do not view these parts as 'unimportant'. Individual children with specific spelling problems are frequently deemed 'lazy'. In reality, the reason this pattern of performance exists is that reading requires only partial cues while spelling requires full information (Frith and Frith 1980). These children read by eye but are forced to spell by ear because they do not abstract the letter-by-letter information of which words are comprised during their reading practice. We still do not have a full explanation of why this is so. However, the case of R.O., a sixteen year-old boy studied by Seymour and MacGregor (1984), suggests that a basic difficulty with visual processing might underlie the deficit.

R.O.'s reading was, on the face of it, normal. He could read regular, irregular and non-words but when words were presented in a vertical rather than a horizontal format, his performance deteriorated dramatically. Thus, R.O. seemed to be able to deal with words holistically but he had difficulty in focusing upon the multi-letter segments of words. While he could manage to read adequately, it can be inferred that his reading style was not conducive to the abstraction of higher-order orthographic 'rules' – the very rules which are required for proficient spelling. Seymour and MacGregor referred to R.O. as a case of 'visual-analytic' dyslexia; to all intents and purposes he resembled one of Frith's group B spellers who have mastered alphabetic skills but failed to pass to the orthographic phase of spelling.

The information we have on the spelling difficulties of dyslexic children is constrained by our models of the spelling process. These are far less sophisticated than their equivalents for the reading process and a great deal more research is needed to further knowledge. Developmentally, the major hurdle is the alphabetic one and dyslexic children who have underlying phonological difficulties will have difficulty in using indirect (non-lexical) spelling routines. They will exhibit a dysphonetic spelling pattern and, by definition, will fail to progress to the orthographic phase although they may possess islets of word-specific knowledge. A second group of children, best described as 'dysgraphic', attain alphabetic skills for spelling yet also fail to move to the orthographic phase. Some may have underlying visual defects while others may rely so heavily upon context during reading that they do not attend in detail to orthographic structure. This style is particularly likely to feature in children whose verbal skills exceed their performance abilities. In the next chapter we shall turn back to examine in detail the vital but also limited role which phonological processing plays in the development of literacy.

6

The importance of phonology

The literature on reading development makes clear that the ability to deal with speech at the level of the phoneme at an early age is a good predictor of later reading achievement. This is because it is necessary to understand the relationship between graphemes and phonemes to make efficient use of an alphabetic reading system. However, transition to the alphabetic phase represents a stumbling block for many dyslexic children who experience phonological difficulties (Frith 1981, 1985). Numbered amongst these are the problems with the organization of auditory information, difficulties with the manipulation and use of phonological memory codes, and difficulties with both speech perception and speech production reviewed in chapter 2. The precise reason for the failure of *individual* children to move to the alphabetic phase of literacy development remains to be established. In principle, it could reside with phonemic awareness, phoneme segmentation or output phonology, or it could be attributable to problems with the use of phonological memory codes.

Ideally, it would be possible to turn to the case literature to throw light upon the question of failure at the individual level. However, interpretation of case studies is complicated because of the emphasis which has been placed upon the reading and spelling processes of subjects during their assessment. We have already alluded to the possibility that individuals who read and spell in the same way may have different underlying deficits. Equally, individuals who read and spell differently may have the same underlying weaknesses.

This is particularly true in cases where there has been re-medial intervention. A child who is basically deficient in phonetic word-attack skills can be taught them. Thereafter this individual's non-word reading could be good – but the child may still be subject to phonological deficits in other areas of functioning. One of the problems encountered when working in the area of developmental disorder is that the pattern of performance with which we are presented may differ from the original state of affairs. This makes it difficult to infer the basis for the problems. No matter what the cause of dyslexia turns out to be, it will be important to take into account underlying patterns of cognitive skill if we are to understand the failure of reading and spelling development.

A developmental analysis of (phonological) dyslexia

To examine how cognitive deficits in dyslexia tie in with reading and spelling profiles, a small group of children were examined, all of whom could be classified as 'developmental phonological dyslexics' because their non-word reading was specifically impaired (Snowling et al. 1986a). We were particularly interested in how, if at all, their pattern of reading and spelling performance linked with their underlying phono-logical skill as assessed by a number of independent tasks. Also we looked in a preliminary way for any changes in reading and spelling style which came about with increasing reading expertise – in some cases through exposure to teaching methods.

The study examined three dyslexics who were reading at the seven-year level and compared them with four dyslexics who had attained a reading age of at least ten years. We were, of course, also interested in the ways in which these dyslexics differed from normal readers and therefore we tested two groups of reading age matched controls, children reading at the seven- and ten-year levels respectively.

In this investigation we looked at the way in which the relationship between cognitive and written language deficits

changed with time, taking Frith's theory of literacy development as a framework. If it is true that the development of
(phonological) dyslexics is arrested within the logographic
phase, we reasoned that a number of predictions about their
reading and spelling behaviour would follow. We thought that
these predictions would be upheld best in dyslexics who had
had the minimum of tutoring (those at reading age seven).
Frith's theory makes less clear predictions about dyslexics
who are better readers and, considering that many of those we
tested had had formal teaching, we expected there to be
variability amongst the group.

Taking the predictions one by one it is possible to see how
well the dyslexics we studied fitted the picture. First we
reasoned that, if the dyslexics were functioning within the
logographic phase, their reading should be inherently inaccurate with a preponderance of visual errors. Moreover, we did
not expect regular words (which normally can be read
phonically) to be read any better than irregular items.
Accordingly we asked our subjects to read aloud a mixed list
of regular and irregular words of one and two syllables. The
normal seven-year-old controls whom we tested showed
a marked 'regularity' effect. On average they read 22 per
cent more regular than irregular words, and 13 per cent of
their reading errors were sound based. For example, they read
pint as 'pinnt' and *vase* as 'vaise'. This suggested that they
already had some alphabetic skill. The ten-year-olds were
generally more proficient. They showed only a slight regular
word advantage (10 per cent) and they made very few errors
overall.

As a group, the dyslexics performed differently from the
controls, particularly at the lower ability level. Two of the
poorer readers, J.M. and T.W., showed a significantly
reduced regularity effect while the other, A.S., was similar to
the controls. She did best on regular words. It was interesting
that she was the oldest of the three and had benefited from the
most remedial help. Our four higher-ability dyslexics performed similarly to their controls. They showed a marginal
advantage for regular words. Thus, the quantitative data

suggested that only J.M. and T.W. were truly within the logographic phase. Error analyses were also significant. Most noticeable in the dyslexic group was an absence of sound-based errors and regularizations. Instead, the majority of the dyslexics' errors were visually based – or logographic. In addition, a substantial proportion were real word responses bearing some visual resemblance to their targets. It will be recalled that such errors were made frequently by the logographic readers studied by Seymour and Elder (1986). The dyslexics also failed to sound out words on a number of occasions (a selection of their errors is shown in table 6.1).

Table 6.1 *Examples of the reading errors made by dyslexic children of reading ages six and seven years*

Logographic	sign/sign	breath/bread
	bowl/blow	cask/cash
	spade/space	pint/pink
Lexical-sounding	flood/fault	lettuce/lettering
	choir/clot	organ/olive
	bleat/built	grill/grit

Source: Snowling et al. (1986a)

Next we looked at non-word reading. A difficulty in this task (compared to reading age matched controls) confirmed the weakness with letter-sound rules suggested by the previous data. However, some qualifications are necessary. Neither J.M. nor T.W. could read any of the nonsense words. The picture was slightly different for the higher reading age dyslexics: one of them, J.N., who attended a specialist school for dyslexic children, managed one-syllable non-words but not two-syllable items as well as controls and it turned out that R.N., who had been tutored, performed within the normal range on our non-word reading tests. Thus, the data from our reading tasks provided evidence for the view that dyslexics have difficulty with alphabetic skills. However, only two of the sample (of lower reading ability) had failed to make any progress towards the alphabetic phase and, at the other end of the scale, two dyslexics were using letter-sound skills quite proficiently, possibly because of the remedial intervention they had received.

Segmentation and spelling skill

The third prediction of Frith's model referred to the spelling processes of dyslexic children. The hypothesis was that their spelling should be weak and that they should have particular difficulty with the use of alphabetic sound-spelling rules. We assumed that these rules would be of most use during the spelling of low frequency, multisyllabic words which the dyslexics had possibly never written before. Therefore we asked them to spell words of one, two and three syllables – and our better readers also attempted four-syllable items.

Overall the dyslexics did less well than reading age matched controls. Furthermore, there was a tendency for their spelling errors to be dysphonetic. Errors included 'fine' for *fish*, 'phins' for *polish*, 'insted' for *instructed* and 'gorhy' for *geography*. This pattern of performance was characteristic of higher reading ability as well as lower reading ability dyslexic subjects. Moreover, a detailed analysis of their errors showed that they were unlike those of normally developing young children who, it will be recalled, make 'semiphonetic' errors. These 'normal' immaturities include the tendency to reduce consonant clusters, to mistranscribe vowels and to omit unstressed syllables. Only about 30 per cent of the dyslexics' errors could be accounted for by such phonological processes. The remaining 70 per cent suggested difficulties due to problems with phoneme segmentation and/or sound-letter translation (see table 6.2 for examples).

To provide further support for this hypothesis, we collected data on phonological processing in tasks other than spelling from our subjects. We administered various auditory proces-

Table 6.2   *Examples of the spelling errors made by low reading age dyslexics*

Normal immaturities	packet/pak
	trumpet/tumput
	finger/fing
	lip/lap
	adventure/adencher
	contented/contened
Segmentation errors	fish/fine
	traffic/tatin
	polish/phins
	instructed/insted
	bump/bunt
	geography/gorhy

Source: Snowling et al. (1986a)

sing tasks, including tests of auditory discrimination, rhyming, syllable and phoneme segmentation, verbal repetition and auditory verbal short-term memory. Here we did anticipate differences within our group as we felt that progress to the alphabetic phase could be hindered for a number of different reasons. Problems with input phonology (auditory perception) would surely slow the acquisition of letter-sound correspondence, problems with phoneme segmentation would have a deleterious effect on spelling and problems with output phonology (pronunciation) might hamper phoneme synthesis or blending processes.

Indeed there was considerable variation in phonological skill. All the dyslexics could segment by syllable but they had difficulty with rhyming tasks and with tasks which required phoneme segmentation. They also had verbal memory deficits. T.W., the most handicapped of our dyslexics (and still within the logographic phase), was the only child to have difficulty with auditory discrimination and just two of the others, J.M. and K.F., had speech difficulties implying deficits at the level of output phonology. While there was variation within the group we were able to show that *all* the dyslexics had problems with phonological tasks and were different from reading age matched controls in this respect. Thus, we were in a good position to argue that deficiencies in phonological processes had caused arrest in reading and spelling development at an early stage. Following arrest it seemed that, for those dyslexics who had progressed, development had been constrained with phonological skills remaining weak, although progress to the alphabetic phase had been possible.

Variation within the syndrome

The earlier one examines a strategy after the point in time at which an impairment has occurred, the more likely it is that the direct influence of that impairment will be detected. According to Frith, entry to the alphabetic phase happens first for spelling and only later are alphabetic skills transferred to reading. We therefore speculated that individual variation in the phonological skills which underlie transition to the alphabetic phase would cause detectable differences in spelling strategy. These would be less apparent when reading was examined.

In an attempt to pick up discernible differences in spelling strategy attributable to phonological deficits, we re-examined the errors made by our lower ability dyslexic readers. Our observations were most enlightening but, before they are reported, it is important to make explicit the nature of the phonological deficits exhibited by the individual children. In brief, T.W. had marked difficulty with input processes and problems throughout the phonological system ensued. A.S. had problems with phoneme segmentation and verbal memory, as did J.M., who in addition had problems with output phonology. The particular pattern of weakness characteristic of each child was reflected in the spelling mistakes he or she made.

To pick out a few examples: T.W. was the most severely

impaired of our subjects in spelling as well as reading. She had more difficulty in writing down the first phoneme of a word than the other dyslexics. When we observed her approach we noticed that she was making use of lip-read information. She tended to write down the last (seen) phoneme first. For example, she wrote *lip* as 'peryse', *tulip* as 'peper'. Moreover, the final phoneme was sometimes confused with another made in the same place in the mouth – hence, she wrote *trap* as 'mupter'. In general her strategy was to get the first phoneme down and then to write out the others where she could, irrespective of their order. It is clear that T.W. had extreme difficulty with phoneme segmentation. She was floored by words of three syllables and the only means she had for tackling them was first to segment by syllable and then to match the syllables with similar sounding words, the spelling of which she knew. Thus, she wrote *catalogue* as 'catofleg', *refreshment* as 'threesleling' and *adventure* as 'hadleguns'. This was perhaps the closest to a logographic strategy that we observed.

A.S. turned out to be a fairly 'typical' example of a dysphonetic, dyslexic speller. Her phoneme segmentation problems were such that she tended to spell the initial parts of words correctly but she had difficulty with the endings. For example, she spelled *traffic* as 'tatin', *nest* as 'nent'. She also made a number of semiphonetic errors, spelling *contented* as 'contintid' and *membership* as 'mabrshep', and her verbal memory problems contributed to the difficulty she had in transcribing three syllable words.

Finally, J.M., who had a history of speech problems and some minor persisting articulation difficulties, was similar in accuracy to A.S. at least when spelling one and two syllable words. However, he had difficulty with the initial parts of words as well as with their endings. His errors were systematic: a particular difficulty with the voicing features of consonants reflected his underlying speech problem. This caused him to spell *sack* as 'sag', *packet* as 'pagit' and *polish* as 'bols'. Also he had great difficulty with three-syllable words, some of which he was unable to pronounce. His attempt for *membership* was 'meaofe' and for *adventure* it was 'afvoerl'. Neither attempt bore much relation to its target.

The individual patterns of spelling performance which our analyses revealed provide grounds for pursuing the idea that both the extent and the severity of a phonological processing deficiency determines the precise nature of the reading and spelling strategies available to a dyslexic person. Let us look for a moment at how the various phonological processes might be used in spelling. By input processes, we refer to the means by which incoming auditory stimuli are registered. We argued that T.W. had a deficit here. This would imply that, for her, input to both a non-lexical sound-letter translation system (the indirect route) and to a direct lexical route would be faulty. Phoneme segmentation is the first step to writing an unfamiliar word and phonological memory is required for the purpose of holding a word in mind while segmenting and sequencing its phonemes. We would argue that all of our dyslexics had difficulty in these processes. Lastly, output phonology will be used when spelling is verbally mediated – a step especially important when spelling unfamiliar words. We thought that J.M. had additional problems here.

Thus, the precise nature of an individual's spelling deficit will depend upon which of the phonological processes are impaired. It follows that children with mild phonological deficits, possibly affecting only one subsystem, should be less handicapped in learning to spell (and read) than children with pervasive phonological disorders. Preliminary evidence comes from a study by Dorothy Bishop of 'dysarthric' children. These are children with known brain damage who cannot control their vocal apparatus in the way which is normally required for speech production. They have circumscribed problems which cause a fairly serious speech disorder. However, in spite of this, Bishop (1985) showed that they could spell proficiently. In contrast, children with phonological disorders which render them unintelligible – but who have no spasticity – have serious spelling difficulties (Robinson et al. 1982), as we shall see in the group of such children studied below.

Reading and spelling in speech-disordered children

In 1983, Joy Stackhouse and I looked at a small group of speech disordered children. Their speech problem was of a 'dyspraxic' nature. This has been defined as a 'phonological disorder resulting from a breakdown in the ability to control the appropriate spatial/temporal properties of speech articulation' (Crary 1984). Incoordination of the vocal tract exists in the absence of paralysis of the speech musculature, or hearing problems. The disorder is most clear-cut in the adult population with acquired neurological problems. Diagnosis is controversial in children where the condition is not as discrete (Williams et al. 1981). There are often associated language and learning problems. The children we studied had received speech therapy and were attending a language unit. They had been unintelligible on starting school and, on testing, they were difficult to understand at times.

Initial investigations were geared towards finding out whether there was any relationship between the speech and the spelling errors made by these children (Snowling and Stackhouse 1983). We therefore asked them to read, to repeat, to spell and to copy a series of one syllable real words. We had intended to use non-word stimuli but, interestingly, these proved to be far too difficult for them to manage. Instead we made use of three-letter words, all containing two consonants and a medial short vowel. Examples included *bun, hat* and *pig*. The dyspraxic subjects attended a language unit within a primary school. They ranged in age from eight to ten years but they were all reading at between the six- and seven-year levels. Hence, we chose as controls younger, normally speaking children from the same school who had reached a similar level of reading attainment. Not surprisingly, the normal controls made fewer errors than the dyspraxics when asked to repeat the experimental words. They were also better at spelling them. The dyspraxic's spelling errors included 'gib' for *gut*, 'nict' for *Nick*, 'tou' for *tub* and 'kin' for *kim*, whereas the normal controls had most difficulty with the representation of vowels.

We proceeded to look at the dyspraxic children's speech errors to see whether these tied in with their spelling mistakes. However, there was no systematic relationship between the two sorts of error. The spelling difficulty of the dyspraxics, like that of the dyslexics we have already discussed, was associated with segmentation problems.

Recently we have followed up this work by looking in detail at two individual dyspraxic children, Michael and Caroline. We were interested to know how they would compare with the sample of dyslexic children who had formed the subjects of our case studies. When we tested him, Michael was eleven years six months old. He was of average intelligence with good spatial ability as evidenced by the British Ability Scales. On starting school, Michael had no verbal communication but, instead, he had used a lot of gesture. When we saw him he was intelligible but marked articulation difficulties were apparent. Caroline was a little older. She was twelve years six months, but again of average intelligence with a similar speech problem. Both she and Michael were reading at the seven years nine months level and their spelling age was six years. They therefore warranted the description 'dyslexic' as well as 'dyspraxic'.

As expected, Michael and Caroline had difficulty on tests of auditory processing and phoneme segmentation. Like many of the other dyslexics we have discussed, they passed auditory discrimination tests but they had problems with rhyming and phoneme segmentation. Verbal repetition was, of course, extremely poor and their verbal memory span was reduced. They could remember four digits presented auditorily and could reverse sequences of a maximum two digits. In this respect they were like the lower reading ability dyslexics, T.W., A.S. and J.M.

It is appropriate to begin by describing Michael and Caroline's spelling performance as it is here that their phonological deficits should have the biggest impact. When asked to spell words of one, two and three syllables, Caroline and Michael did less well than any of the other phonological dyslexics we have studied, with the exception of T.W., who was, the most handicapped. Very few of their errors were normal phonological immaturities but rather they reflected segmentation problems. What was interesting was that each child had adopted a different strategy to deal with the task of spelling by ear.

First let us look at Michael. Michael wrote *sack* as 'sata', *puppy* as 'pats' and *traffic* as 'tarres'. He sometimes 'searched' for phonemes, making obvious mouth movements whilst doing so – and every sound he stumbled upon he wrote down. For *trumpet* he wrote 'trpbbie' and when attempting *trap* he searched for /tr/ writing first 'the', then 'we', then he searched for /p/ writing 'n' then 'm' then 't'. The resulting 'thewenmt' was way off target. Michael's searching behaviour was most marked when he was presented with three syllable words (see table 6.3). At first glance his errors seem bizarre and unsystematic. However, careful analysis suggests that Michael was trying quite hard to segment these words. His attempts were complicated because he tended to back-track

Table 6.3 *Spellings of three-syllable words by two children with phonological disorder*

Target spelling	Michael	Caroline
membership	mabsttb mabspht splt sthp	bnbship
September	sabarber smber	september
cigarette	satesatarhaelerari	silonwet
umbrella	rberhertelrarlsrllles	umber umturd
understand	rarato sandrarde	undercellow
refreshment	lpohet	withfirstmint
adventure	arterer	andbackself
catalogue	catcolg catdog gog	catanlog
instructed	hisokder	indivrd
contented	kitr	contartit

and approach again segments with which he was unhappy. To illustrate, *understand* has three syllables: /un/, /der/, /stand/. Michael had two attempts at the first, producing 'rara', followed by an attempt at the second, 'to', and the third, 'sand', respectively. He then went back to the first twice, 'ra', 'r', and on to the second, 'de'. His final spelling was 'raratosandrarde'. His attempt of 'rberhertelrarlsrllles' for *umbrella* can be similarly deciphered: 'r' was an attempt at the first syllable, 'berh' and 'er' two attempts at the second, and 'tel' his first shot at the third. The back-tracking then began with 'ra' for the first, 'rl' for the second, 'sr' for the third syllable. Finally he tried 'lll' for the second and 'es' for the third!

Michael's spell-by-phoneme strategy was less than effective, perhaps in part because of his pronunciation problems. Caroline's spelling attempts also reflected a tendency to search for segments but she did this to a lesser extent then Michael. The instances we noted were 'duidry' for *trumpet*, both 'dui' and 'dry' being attempts at the first syllable, and 'bybrdwn' for *polish* comprising three different attempts at the first syllable: 'by', 'br' and 'dwn'.

There was a major difference between the spelling of Caroline and Michael. Caroline did not persist with the ineffective spell-by-phoneme strategy. Instead, and particularly with three-syllable words, she began to spell using word components. Thus she spelled *catalogue* as 'catanlog', *adventure* as 'andbackself' and refreshment as 'withfirstmint'. It will be recalled that this strategy was used to some extent by T.W. It was as though both girls could perceive 'word-shape' but could not reflect upon phonemic structure.

Thus, the spelling of both Michael and Caroline was seriously impaired as a result of their phonological difficulties. It follows that their reading must have been arrested within the logographic phase. Indeed this was true. They did as poorly on tests of regular, irregular and non-word reading as lower reading age dyslexics, although it is important to point out that their reading errors were different. Fifty-two per cent of Michael's reading errors, and 38 per cent of Caroline's,

were visually similar to their targets and at least one of these
for each child bore a semantic resemblance. *Lime* was read as
'lemon', *aunt* as 'uncle' and *prince* as 'Princess Anne'. The
remaining errors were mainly unsuccessful attempts to apply
letter-sound rules. Some 42 per cent of Michael's errors were
like this, some 59 per cent of Caroline's. The error rate in both
cases exceeded that of the dyslexics to whom we had
administered the same tests (see figure 6.1). A likely
explanation was that the application of alphabetic rules was
compromised in the dyspraxics because of their phonological
output difficulties. In short, when they attempted to decode
words by sound, they had specific problems with sound-
blending and their own faulty articulation was prone to send
them awry. Difficulties with phoneme synthesis led Caroline
for example, to read *command* as 'cabinet' and *temper* as
'chemist'. The problem was serious because she accepted her
own readings as correct and therefore was in danger of
increasing the disorder within her lexical system.

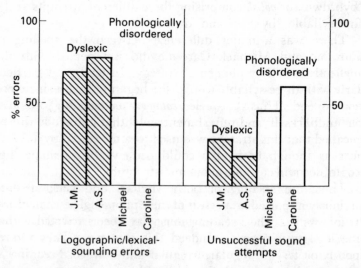

Figure 6.1. *Distribution of logographic and lexical-sounding errors to
unsuccessful sound attempts in dyslexic readers and reading age matched
children with phonological disorder*

If Michael and Caroline can be regarded as typical of children who have serious phonological disabilities, then such children are both similar to and different from phonological dyslexics. They are similar in that literacy development has been arrested within the logographic phase but different in that their phonological difficulties are pervasive to an extent which may well preclude the development of literacy along normal lines. At the time that Michael and Caroline were tested their spelling was grossly impaired and they had significant decoding difficulties despite several years of good remedial teaching emphasizing phonic methods. To an extent they had learned letter-sound correspondences but they could not apply them in spelling because of segmentation difficulties or in reading because of problems with sound blending.

The argument developed so far in this chapter is that the extent and indeed the severity of a child's phonological difficulty will in large part dictate the course of reading and spelling development he or she follows. However, as will be seen in the next section, phonology is not all that is required if literacy is to be achieved.

Surface dyslexia in a child who could read well?

To hold that phonological skills are crucial for the acquisition of reading and spelling processes, is by no means new. Jorm and Share (1983), for example, have argued that individual differences in phonological processing are the major source of differences in reading achievement. According to their view, phonological recoding strategies function as a self-teaching mechanism for children and they are also important for reading comprehension. Specifically, they are needed to hold items which have been decoded for later integration, and for storing sentence context in working memory so that it can facilitate word identification. To the extent that they are subject to phonological deficits, disabled readers will be at a disadvantage.

While the ideas of Jorm and Share ring true, we must be cautious, for on the other side of the coin, the possession of adequate phonological skill does not ensure that reading and spelling will be successfully acquired. To an extent, superior decoding can be a hindrance as we shall see in the case of Diana, a bilingual child who had for many years masked a considerable reading difficulty.

Linda Pring and I first met Diana when we were carrying out our experiments on the effect of semantic context on word recognition (Pring and Snowling 1986). Diana was notable because she did not appear to be subject to the semantic facilitation effect: semantically related primes did not appear to speed up her reading of single word targets. In fact, when we examined her data there was an effect of context – but one which was smaller than that characteristic of the other children in our study. This led us to look in detail at her reading skill which, it turned out, had been worrying her teachers for some time.

When we tested Diana she was eleven years nine months old. Considering that she was in a mainstream classroom, we were surprised to find that her Full Scale W.I.S.C.-R. I.Q. was 67 – a score which placed her within the 'borderline' range for children who require special education. Diana gained equivalent scores for the Verbal and Performance items. She scored at the fifth centile on Raven's Matrices and her Verbal Mental Age equivalent was five years three months according to the British Picture Vocabulary Scale, a test of receptive vocabulary. She also did poorly on T.R.O.G., a test which measures the ability to understand grammatical constructions (Bishop 1982). We learned that Diana's parents were Armenian Cypriots and that the language of the home was Armenian. However, she conversed easily with us in English and she had never been considered to require English as a second language teaching.

Diana's reading skill was much higher than her abilities in other spheres might suggest. Her reading age was reported by her teacher to be at least twelve years but we decided to begin by asking her to read a series of regular and irregular words to explore her use of visual and phonological reading strategies (Coltheart et al. 1983). Diana's reading of the regular words was perfect. However, she misread many of the irregular items. There were twelve reading errors altogether, seven of them

Table 6.4 *Reading errors made by Diana, an advanced 'decoder', when reading aloud irregular words*

Regularizations	gauge/gorge
	scarce/[skɑs]
	subtle/[sʌbtʌl]
	debt/[dɛbt]
	mortgage/[mɒtgeɪdʒ]
	trough/[troʊ]
	circuit/[sərkʊt]
Partial failures of grapheme-phoneme rules	gross/grass
	duel/dwell
	spear/spare
	protein/[proʊtɪn]

being regularizations and the remainder, partial failures of grapheme-phoneme rules (see table 6.4). Thus, Diana appeared to be relying upon letter-sound rules in her reading and this was borne out by her non-word decoding which was perfect. She also made very few errors on Coltheart's test of silent homophone matching, a test in which word pairs have to be sorted according to whether they sound the same, as for example *bear/bare*, or sound different, *bear/beer*. She did equally well where the word pairs were regular, irregular or non-words.

Diana's decoding of single words was certainly excellent, but her understanding of what she read was less good. She gave correct definitions for only nineteen of the twenty seven homophones which she could read aloud. On four occasions, she confused the meaning of one homophone with that of another. For instance, she defined *stake* as 'meat', *bare* as 'polar bear', *brake* as 'you break a vase' and *tale* as 'crocodile has a tail'. In three further cases her definitions were incorrect. She defined *claws* as 'a horse has claws', *bowled* as 'when you mix a cake' and *daze* as 'to watch with your eyes'. We explored the hypothesis that Diana had a semantic deficit using a task devised by Funnell (1983). Presented with a printed word, let's say *orange*, she had to choose which one of two further words most closely matched it for meaning – say, *lemon* or *tangerine*. Diana's only mistakes were to pair *ladle* with *fork* rather than *spoon* and *tack* with *screw* rather than *nail*. Granted we do not have the appropriate control data but, with so few errors on this test, and also on a semantic categorization task of our own devising, we did not pursue this possibility any further. Instead we decided to examine Diana's reading beyond the single word level guided by the observation that she had been unperturbed by any of the reading errors she had made.

We therefore presented Diana with sentences containing homographs. These are printed words which have ambiguous pronunciations such as *row*, *minute*, *lead* and *bow* (Frith and Snowling 1983). The pronunciation of a homograph is usually made clear by the sentence in which it is embedded. So, *lead* is pronounced to rhyme with 'bed' in the sentence *the scrap metal man collected the lead* but to rhyme with *feed* in the sentence *the man took his dog out on the lead*. Diana, however, did not pay attention to sentence context – she gave the most frequent pronunciation of the homograph concerned, regardless of its meaning in the sentence.

To explore Diana's reading comprehension further she was presented with a nature story in which one appropriate word had to be isolated from two inappropriate words (all of the same syntactic class) at intervals throughout the text. An example would be the sentence *The beaver sniffed the air and cut a --- branch from a tree*, where the choice was between the words *small*, *red* and *liquid* to complete the gap. In this example, Diana chose *liquid* and over the test as a whole she made twelve out of eighty-eight implausible responses. These occurred equally often for choices including nouns, verbs, adjectives and prepositions. Not surprisingly, Diana had great difficulty answering questions about what she had read. Neither her word selections nor her responses to comprehension questions were as accurate as those of normal readers who read at the eight year level (Snowling and Frith 1986). It will be recalled that Diana's decoding skill was much better than this.

Thus we established that Diana's reading difficulty was

primarily one of reading comprehension, and it was probably linked with a more general language disability. In contrast, her phonological skills were normal and it is worth mentioning that her verbal memory was good (as were visual memory skills). We were of the opinion that Diana's reading development had been fostered by her ability to learn and to use spelling-sound correspondences. Certainly she had passed through into the alphabetic phase of development. Moreover, her expertise with irregular words, although not without fault, indicated that she possessed a good deal of word-specific, lexical knowledge.

Diana's proficiency with alphabetic skill and her relative difficulty with irregular words was mirrored in her spelling performance. Her spelling of regular words was excellent but she failed to spell seven of the irregular words which she had also failed to read. She had difficulty with only two words. which she had read correctly. These were *castle* which she wrote as 'casctle' and *answer* which she spelled as 'aunswer'. In both these cases, Diana included silent letters, thereby revealing definite word-specific knowledge. So, unlike the phonological dyslexics we have studied, Diana was a 'phonetic' speller. She produced virtually perfect renderings of the three syllable regular words used by Snowling et al. (1986a) and all her errors were phonetically accurate. For example, she spelled *cigarette* as 'ciggarette' and *catalogue* as 'cataloge'.

Our evidence is by no means complete, but what we have available suggests that Diana was functioning within the alphabetic phase of literacy development and, in addition, she had substantial word-specific knowledge. In this respect she resembled some of the developmental surface or morphemic dyslexics who have been described in the literature. Importantly, Diana had language comprehension difficulties and a greatly reduced spoken vocabulary for her age. So although her phonological strategies for reading and spelling were good, she was *not* a good reader. As a consequence of her language problems, Diana tended to misread irregular words, often producing nonsensical responses or 'neologisms', such as 'mortgauge'; she was unperturbed when she read aloud sentences which did not make sense; and she had poor understanding of what she read. We might speculate that Diana had only registered orthographically, printed words for which she already had a semantic representation. There was a subset of words which she could neither read nor spell and, although we did not ask Diana to define them, it is highly unlikely that she would have been able to do so.

The hypothesis which emerges from Diana's case is that transition to the orthographic phase proper is contingent upon semantic factors. As yet we do not have enough information to specify the mechanism. What is important for present purposes is that, in spite of the overwhelming importance of phonology to reading development, on its own it does not guarantee reading success. The reading difficulties of children who have intact phonological skill are quite different from those of children with phonological deficits, as chapter 7 will show.

7

Hyperlexia

Just as 'dyslexia' refers to unexpected reading failure, so 'hyperlexia' means surprising reading success. Hyperlexic children read at a much higher level than is to be anticipated considering their age and intelligence. They are usually mentally retarded and many of the reported cases have had autistic features (Mehegan and Dreyfuss 1972; Elliott and Needleman 1976; Whitehouse and Harris 1984). Against this background of developmental disorder and (usually) language delay, the reading achievement of hyperlexic children is outstanding. Some hyperlexics have learned to read before they were three years old and certainly many have done so prior to formal instruction. What is it about them that permits such rapid and effortless acquisition of the skill that more intelligent dyslexic children cannot easily master?

Before beginning to answer this question, it is necessary to discuss the nature of hyperlexic reading. The general impression gleaned from the literature is well summarized by Healy (1982): '[hyperlexics show] flawless oral reading followed by the total inability to demonstrate comprehension either by retelling or answering questions.' However, we need to know more precisely which strategies these 'good' readers possess and which, if any, are absent from their repertoire; a psycholinguistic analysis of their reading processes is required.

Single-word reading in hyperlexia

In a school run by the National Society for Autistic Children, Uta Frith and I came across nine children who were exceptionally good readers. These children fitted the only criteria for 'hyperlexia' which existed at the time. They were said by their teachers to 'bark at print', and this statement presented a challenge to us. We knew that autistic children usually have intact visual-perceptual skill and that their verbal memory tends to be good. However, they typically perform on cognitive tasks as though unaware of structure and meaning (Hermelin and O'Connor 1970). We wondered therefore if their reading was accomplished through superior pattern recognition. In principle, word shapes could have been linked with word names through repeated association. Cobrinik (1982) made a similar suggestion after showing that a group of nine hyperlexic boys was better at deciphering degraded familiar words than normal readers.

Now, if hyperlexic reading is merely 'barking at print' and autistic children learn words one by one by memorizing their shapes and sounds, their reading skill should not be generalizable. They should not be able to decipher novel words and they should not find regular words any easier to read (via a phonic method) than irregular ones. Furthermore, there is no reason why concrete words should be read more easily than abstract items, unless of course it is these words to which they have been exposed. We decided to test these predictions systematically (Frith and Snowling 1983). Moreover, if hyperlexic children do not access meaning from printed words we reasoned that they would not be susceptible to the 'Stroop effect'. This classic effect, named after its originator, occurs in colour naming tasks where there is interference from printed words. A person's ability to name colours can be readily measured by timing their responses to series of coloured crosses (xxxx). Now, it takes extra time for them to name the colours of the ink in which conflicting colour words are written – like the word *blue* written in red, where the correct response is 'red'. This extra time is an estimation of 'Stroop Interference'. The Stroop effect is reliable; it affects adults and children from the time they start to read, and it occurs because word reading is faster than colour naming.

In our initial experiments, we compared the performance of our hyperlexic subjects with that of reading age matched controls but, before doing this, we administered a battery of standardized reading tests to ensure that we were on the right track. One of these was the Neale Analysis of Reading Ability, a test in which short passages are read and questions about them answered. This is a test we administer routinely to dyslexic children and we were struck by the marked difference in the way our hyperlexics performed. It was just as though 'hyperlexia' and 'dyslexia' were two sides of the same coin. Whereas dyslexics frequently stumble through the passages yet have surprisingly good comprehension of what they read, the hyperlexics sped through them but had surprisingly bad comprehension. It was because of this observation that we included in our study a small group of dyslexic children whose reading accuracy was the same as that of hyperlexics.

We started by asking our subjects to read aloud lists of concrete and abstract words which were matched for frequency of occurrence. All our subjects, hyperlexic, dyslexic or normal readers, read concrete words faster and with fewer errors than abstract words. There was no difference whatsoever between the groups with regard to this word dimension. So, we could rule out the possibilty that the hyperlexics had learned an arbitrary system of visual-verbal associations. For them, the lexical representation of abstract and concrete words was evidently the same as that of reading age matched controls. We next went on to examine their use of phonological reading strategies.

We did this in two ways. First subjects read lists containing regular words such as *treat* and *dance*, and irregular words such as *aunt* and *break* which were matched for frequency. Second, they read difficult lists of two-syllable non-words such as *brigbert* and *tegwop*. On both tests, the hyperlexics performed exactly like normal controls – they read regular words better than irregular ones and they had no specific difficulty with the non-word items. It was in fact the dyslexics who showed deficiencies. In line with previous work, we found that their non-word reading was impaired and the advantage of regular over irregular words was absent from their data. An obvious hypothesis was that hyperlexics learn to read easily because of intact phonological skills, whilst dyslexics have difficulty because of weaknesses within this system.

Lastly, we administered a Stroop test. We presented the children with cards bearing rows of coloured circles containing either printed colour words (red, blue, green) or a series of crosses (xxx). They had to name, as quickly as possible, the colours of the ink in which the circles were printed. In the experimental condition, the name of the colour word printed inside the circle conflicted with the actual colour of the circle. For example, the word *red* might be printed inside a *blue* circle. The target response would be *blue*. In the classic Stroop effect it takes longer to name the colour under these circumstances than when it is paired with a neutral stimulus such as the crosses in the control condition. It can be assumed that naming time is slowed because of interference from the meaning of the incongruent colour word which conflicts.

All our subjects performed similarly on this test, exhibiting a clear Stroop effect. This suggested that, just like normal readers, hyperlexics could access the meaning of the colour words they read. A possible objection is that the interference occurred because the colour words were more distracting than the crosses – and not because of their meaning. So we have since extended this initial observation by asking our hyperlexics to name the colours of circles containing verbal stimuli of different classes: incongruent colour words as before (red, blue, green), the names of colours other than those used as inks in the experiment (pink, black, orange), unrelated words (door, table, house), pronounceable non-words (*pilt, reft, laice*); or strings of crosses. As the semantic similarity between the target colour name and the name of the interfering stimulus increased, the longer it took our subjects to name the colour of the ink. This finding, known as the *semantic gradient effect* (Klein 1964) indicates unequivocally that they were extracting meaning from the colour words they were reading (see figure 7:1). Thus, hyperlexic reading is more than 'barking at print'. Hyperlexic readers can recognize words using visual-orthographic and phonological strategies and they can read non-words proficiently (see also Healy et al. 1982; Siegal 1984). They also show the usual effects of word frequency and imageability. In short, their processing of printed words was normal, at least at single-word level.

We also looked at their decoding in connected prose. When reading aloud, hyperlexic reading sounds strange as punctuation tends to be ignored or misplaced (Goldberg and Rothermel 1984) and hyperlexics do not read with intonation. Nonetheless we found that their *decoding* in these circumstances was normal, at least according to a sentence completion task. In English, final *s* is pronounced /s/ after a consonant as in *dogs* but /z/ after a vowel as in *vase*. We presented subjects

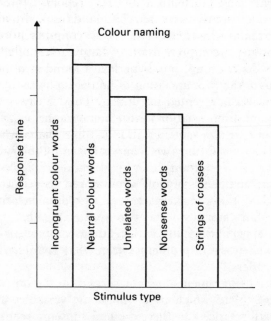

Figure 7.1. *Semantic gradient effect*

with sentences containing non-words. These non-words were marked as singular or plural according to their position in the sentence. In the sentence, *two bippes left the town*, the *s* should be pronounced /z/ because *bippes* is plural. In the sentence *a teffes knocked on the door*, the *s* should be pronounced /s/ because *teffes* is singular. This is in fact what the hyperlexic children did. They were just a sensitive as normal children to this particular syntactic distinction and their pronunciation of the stimuli reflected their knowledge. Until this point we had found that hyperlexics performed exactly like reading age matched controls. We next moved to examine their understanding of what they read.

Comprehension beyond single-word level

Beyond the single-word level, hyperlexics fare less well. Huttenlocher and Huttenlocher (1973) reported three cases who responded poorly to written commands and, although the subjects examined by Healy et al. (1982) comprehended short literal sentences, comprehension of larger units of text was very poor. As a group, our hyperlexics found it difficult to disambiguate the pronunciation of homographs such as *bow*, *lead*, which were presented in context. They always gave the most frequent pronunciation for the homographs regardless of their meaning in the sentence and, just like Diana whom we described chapter 6, they were unperturbed by their mispronunciations. In addition, they had more difficulty than reading age matched controls when asked to select one of three words of the same syntactic class to complete sentences within a short story. So the two results together pointed towards a specific difficulty with reading comprehension – a deficit which was quite different from that characteristic of dyslexic readers.

Our initial experiments had one serious limitation. We had set out to explore which psycholinguistic variables affected reading performance and therefore had chosen a reading age match design. All well and good. But when we wished to ask *why* hyperlexics were failing to comprehend, we could not answer this question to our satisfaction because seven of the nine hyperlexics were retarded while all the normal readers (and all the dyslexics) were at least of average intelligence. Hence, we were obliged to design a second series of experiments in which we compared a larger group: this time sixteen 'hyperlexic', autistic adolescents, all reading at the eight year level, with a group of mildly retarded school leavers who were of similar mental as well as reading age. We also included as controls a group of younger normal children matched for reading age (Snowling and Frith 1986). This design allowed us to enquire into the role of verbal intelligence in reading comprehension and also, incidentally, to establish whether 'hyperlexia' was an autism-specific phenomenon.

Some general findings emerged from our study and it is worth stating these at the outset. First, among handicapped groups (autistic and retarded non-autistic children), verbal ability was the best predictor of reading comprehension. Handicapped children, regardless of diagnostic group, whose mental age was above seven years, could comprehend just as well as younger reading age matched controls, and their comprehension processes were, to this extent, normal. Children with a verbal mental age of below seven years were more typically 'hyperlexic'. They read without apparent understanding and their comprehension was poorer than that of normally developing readers whose mental age was equally low.

These results have made us cautious about application of the label 'hyperlexia'. Previously terminology in this area have been vague. A suggestion by Healy (1982) was that the term should be applied only to cases of children who, as well as having higher decoding than comprehension skill, have manifested the early development of reading. We would wish to make a further restriction, that the term should be reserved for individuals who show both unexpected decoding success *and* surprising comprehension failure – the surprise being in relation to verbal ability.

Two of our experiments (Experiments 3 and 4) make our

reasons plain. In these experiments, we asked subjects to read nature stories which had been revised in various ways. We were interested in finding out how well the hyperlexic readers could understand the individual sentences and also whether they would be able to follow the story as a whole. We therefore embedded tests of individual sentence and overall text processing within the stories. At the end, we also asked questions to test the children's understanding of what they had read. We used a modified cloze procedure so that, at intervals throughout a lengthy text, the children had to choose one out of three words to complete a gap. The three words were always of the same grammatical class but their appropriateness was manipulated systematically. One alternative fitted both the sentence and the story context. We called this the *story-appropriate* choice. Another alternative fitted the sentence but not the story context. This was the *sentence-appropriate* choice. Finally, an *inappropriate* choice fitted neither the story nor the sentence context.

An example will make our design clearer. Take the sentence *their mother/friends/room led the young beavers to the pond*. The choice between *mother* and *friends* depended upon the text as a whole. Both would have been plausible completions but, in this story, *mother* happened to be correct. Thus, *mother* was *story-appropriate*, *friends* was *sentence-appropriate*. The third possibility, *room* was semantically implausible – it fitted neither sentence nor story context. We reasoned that a preference for *story-appropriate* items would signal efficient text processing over and above sentence level. If *inappropriate* items were not systematically rejected, this would signal a failure of comprehension of even small units of meaning within the sentence.

As already hinted, the handicapped children of higher verbal ability (some ten years) performed as well as reading age matched controls. They all rejected inappropriate words and showed a definite preference for story-appropriate choices. So not only were they able to integrate word meanings at sentence level but also they were integrating the meanings of the individual sentences over the text as a whole. This was not the case for the lower ability handicapped children who performed less well than normally developing controls. However, contrary to the notion that 'hyperlexics' read without understanding, even the low ability subjects (whose mental age was on average six years) showed some sign of comprehension. They could all reject implausible choices which were, of course, semantically incongruous with the rest of the sentence in which they were placed. What they apparently could not do was to follow the story as a whole, and therefore they did not differentiate between sentence-appropriate and story-appropriate choices.

One problem with an 'on-line' comprehension task of the type we used is that subjects may perform better than is usually the case because they have their attention drawn explicitly to the selections of words. Thus, text processing can be artificially enhanced. We thought that this might well explain the seemingly good comprehension, at least at sentence level, of the hyperlexics. So we devised a second task in which subjects again read aloud a story, but this time we surreptitiously embedded anomalous words in the text. The subjects' task was to strike out any of these words which they were able to detect. For example, in the sentence *the hedgehog could smell the scent of electric flowers*, the word *electric* is implausible and therefore should have been cancelled out.

Once again, the performance of higher verbal ability, handicapped subjects was indistinguishable from that of controls. They found the implausible words easily. In contrast, the children of lower verbal ability were unsuccessful. They simply could not do the task and ended up by striking out as many perfectly acceptable words as anomalous targets, in some cases many more. When monitoring was not enforced as it had been by the cloze-like procedure, their comprehension of what they read was minimal. They read on, quite unperturbed by the silliness of what they were saying.

It is worth emphasizing that the lower ability 'hyperlexics' performed less well than higher ability handicapped children and *also* less well than normal readers of similarly low mental age. Despite their relatively low scores on the vocabulary test, low ability normal readers had resources which allowed them to detect implausible words in stories, both when attention was drawn to them, and to a degree, when it was not. Furthermore, they chose story-appropriate over sentence-appropriate alternatives, revealing an ability to process text at story level.

Comprehension in 'hyperlexia'

Text comprehension can be enhanced by the way the reader integrates 'old' information already in his or her mind with 'new' information the text provides. We devised a simple test of what our subjects had gleaned from the texts they had read by asking two types of question. One required specific factual details to be recalled from the sentences, the other invited the use of general knowledge about the topic of the stories. One of the *fact* questions, for example, was: 'For how long had the hedgehog been in her underground nest?' The correct answer was 'three months' and this could only have been given had specific details from the text been remembered. One of the *general knowledge* questions was: 'What makes hedgehogs wake up from their winter sleep?' While the answer to this question was given in the text, it is conceivable that readers could have answered it on the basis of the knowledge that hibernating animals wake up in spring. Indeed, we found that normal readers of the same reading level as our experimental subjects could answer many of the general knowledge questions without actually reading the texts. They could not do this in the case of the questions tapping story-facts.

The performance of normal readers who had *not* read the stories gave us objective grounds for distinguishing between *fact* and *general knowledge* questions. Our higher ability subjects made this distinction too for they answered general knowledge questions better than story-factual ones. They were exactly similar to reading age matched controls in this respect. We were able to conclude that *all* our normal readers and the handicapped children of mental age greater than seven years could use general knowledge to supplement their memory for, and we presume understanding of, a text. In contrast, lower ability 'hyperlexic' readers did not do this. Their ability to answer *general knowledge* questions was as poor as their ability to recall factual information from the texts. Moreover, they did worse on both types of question than a group of pre-readers whose mental ages ranged from just three years six months to four years five months.

Probably the best conclusion we can reach, given our results, is that truly 'hyperlexic' readers process texts superficially and remember only isolated details from them. We would argue that they do not access pre-existing knowledge during reading – if indeed they possess this knowledge. The consequence is that new facts are not well represented and stories cannot generally be understood.

What is 'hyperlexia'?

We believe that the results of these experiments are important for several reasons. First, none of them revealed deficits specific to autistic children. In every case, the performance of autistic children was the same as that of mental age matched controls who were also slow learners. Second, although all the handicapped children showed remarkable decoding skill, they did not all merit the label 'hyperlexia'. The comprehension of autistic and mildly retarded children whose mental age was above seven years was entirely as to be predicted, given their age and verbal intelligence. Therefore their reading development could be said to be normal, taking into account the slower than average rate at which they have acquired other cognitive skills. Moreover, there is nothing magical about the mental age of seven years. It happened to be a cut-off in the present study because of the reading level of the texts we had devised.

In contrast, the reading comprehension of lower verbal ability handicapped children was *worse* than that of matched normal readers. They therefore could uneqivocally be described as 'hyperlexic'. Diana, it will be recalled, had a mental age of around five years and she also had trouble in understanding these texts. She therefore warrants the same 'diagnosis'. Interestingly, both in her case and in the case of the 'hyperlexics' in our experiments, reading failure was evident only beyond the single word level. Thus, the very existence of 'hyperlexia' demonstrates that, in principle, a functional decoding system can be set up in the absence of the usual links with the semantic or general knowledge systems. By investigating hyperlexic children, we can gain insight into the benefit which these links might have.

We have spoken about the links between the cognitive and the reading system before. It is mainly these links which account for the use of context in reading. If unskilled readers characteristically rely more heavily upon context than proficient readers (Stanovich 1980), it could be that these links provide a vital resource for dyslexic children. We have alluded to the fact that dyslexics and 'hyperlexics' are like two sides of a coin. Could it be that, while 'hyperlexics' hide their reading difficulty by virtue of their excellent decoding skill, dyslexics make use of cognitive skills, normal or even good comprehension in particular, to compensate for their decoding deficit? Chapter 8 returns to the question of dyslexia and considers the interplay of strengths and weakesses in the development of dyslexic children.

8

Proficiency and deficiency: the interplay of strengths and weaknesses in dyslexia

In the previous chapters we have seen that many dyslexic children have phonological difficulties. However, in spite of their problems, dyslexic children can and do learn to read. How do they accomplish a level of literacy which initially seems beyond them?

When a child fails to progress because of a constitutional weakness, there are at least two ways in which development might proceed. If the weakness is by its nature an immaturity, then the child will gradually mature. Development will be slow but nevertheless along normal lines. This is usually known as *developmental delay*. However, if development has been arrested because of a specific deficit rather than an immaturity, it might be necessary for the child to adopt compensatory strategies. In this case development will follow an alternative course and, when this happens, we usually speak of a *developmental disorder*. Now, if we maintain that classically dyslexia comes about because of a failure to progress to the alphabetic phase of literacy development, there will be a number of children who move forward by gradually improving their phonological skill. Among these, some will do so slowly but spontaneously, while for others progress will come about through remedial teaching. Furthermore, it is likely that some dyslexics, maybe the majority, learn to read using compensatory strategies, like those discussed below.

Achieving literacy with a phonological deficit

Let us begin by discussing the interesting case of R.E. reported by Campbell and Butterworth (1985). R.E. was a student at university when she was studied and, although she had a history of dyslexia, she had learned to read and to spell exceedingly well – in fact as well as her undergraduate peers. Nonetheless, R.E.'s pattern of performance was such that she could be called phonologically dyslexic – she read real words well but had problems finding pronunciations for letters or graphemic units and she read only 60 per cent of non-words correctly. She was also dysgraphic. The spelling errors which she made were non-phonetic and her difficulties were associated with deficits in phonemic awareness and phonological processing.

Although literate, R.E. could be classified as a 'developmental phonological dyslexic'. While her ability to categorize phonemes was normal, she performed below the level to be expected on tests of phoneme segmentation. She could not count the phonemes in words very well and her auditory rhyme judgements were impaired. In fact R.E. admitted that she could not 'hear' the 'little sounds' in words – she could not reflect upon the phonological structure of what she could adequately hear.

A central feature of R.E.'s dyslexic condition was a marked verbal memory deficit. Her memory span was confined to four digits which she could repeat equally well backwards as forwards. Regardless of list length, her memory for visually presented material was better than her auditory recall and consequently she would rely upon visual memory resources whenever it was feasible to do so. Campbell and Butterworth argued that R.E. had been unable to learn spelling–sound correspondences because the auditory component of short-term memory could not support phonemic parsing processes.

Thus she had not mastered the alphabetic principle but literacy had been achieved and it is probable that her visual skills had supported development.

Until now we have mainly been concerned with a simple two-route model of reading where familiar words are read by a visually-based lexical process and novel words are handled by a non-lexical phonological system (figure 4.2 routes C and D, p. 48). However, Glushko (1979) and also Marcel (1980b) have claimed that a purely lexical process of activation and synthesis can account for non-word as well as real word reading. The process envisaged is one where any perceived novel letter-string is segmented in all possible ways, each segment accessing matching segments in the visual lexicon (a system arranged along orthographic lines). The pronunciation of new strings is thought to be synthesized by the amalgamation of the different pronunciations active throughout the network. The time to synthesize a pronunciation will be less where all the active pronunciations are consistent (e.g. *mash, dash, sash, cash*) than when there are some inconsistent neighbours (e.g. *maid, laid, said*). Thus, if non-words are read according to a purely alphabetic process of letter-sound translation, it should take an equivalent amount of time to read the novel strings *heaf* and *heak*. However, Glushko found that it took longer to pronounce the non-word *heaf* because of the influence of the neighbours *deaf* and *leaf* which have different pronunciations than to read *heak* where all the neighbours, e.g. *beak, teak, leak* have the same pronunciation.

Campbell and Butterworth pointed out that R.E. may have been able to use lexical analogies even though she could not effectively use grapheme-phoneme correspondences proficiently. Hence, if she could read *moth*, she could have learned to synthesize pronunciations for *froth* and *broth* while they were still novel to her by virtue of their orthographic similarity. Analogic mappings make less stringent demands on a phonemic parsing system than do grapheme-phoneme rules and therefore they could have provided an alternative means for learning to read.

Orthographic priming and dyslexia

The case of R.E. raises a new possibility; at least some dyslexic individuals might learn to read without passing through the alphabetic phase in the 'normal way'. That is, without being able to segment at the phonemic level. The hypothesis entailed is that such readers will decipher the novel words they encounter not by grapheme-phoneme conversion but by a visual process of lexical activation and synthesis in which the similarity between a new word and a previously seen item provides the basis for reading by analogy. To take an example: the novel string *racht* can be pronounced 'rached' by grapheme-phoneme conversion, but an analogic process would more likely produce the pronunciation 'rot', by analogy with 'yacht'. If it is true that dyslexics can use a system of lexical analogies, it should be possible to show that their non-word reading is subject to a lexical influence.

One of the most straightforward ways of looking for a lexical influence on non-word reading was devised by Kay and Marcel (1981). They used a priming procedure in which non-words were preceded by real words which shared the same orthographic segments, for example *heaf* preceded by *deaf*. Using this paradigm, they were able to bias the pronunciations of the same critical segments within the non-words. Thus, having seen *deaf*, adults were more likely to pronounce *heaf* as 'heff' than if they had previously seen an orthographically dissimilar word. On the other hand, having seen *leaf*, subjects were more likely to give the pronunciation 'heef'. It was known from the work of Campbell (1985) that children are susceptible to a lexical priming effect, at least in spelling. Therefore, Marcia Williams and I decided to use Kay and Marcel's procedure to see whether it was possible to influence the non-word reading of dyslexic children (unpublished).

In our experiment we tested ten dyslexics aged twelve years who were reading at the nine and a half year level and compared their performance to that of reading age matched controls. We chose a lexical decision task in which a list of single syllable stimuli comprising regular and irregular words, plus non-words, all of the same orthographic structure (*moth/both/coth*) was presented. Thus, the non-words differed from the real word items only by the first letter. They were preceded either by an orthographically related regular (*moth*), irregular (*both*) or neutral (*bull*) prime. We wanted to know whether the children's pronunciations would be biased by the primes, so we told them that some of the letter strings would be 'nonsense'. Having found a nonsense word they should read it aloud.

As expected given our reading age matching procedure, dyslexic and normal readers did not differ in their performance on the real word items and, in line with previous work, we found that dyslexics made more errors in non-word reading than controls. Our new finding was that dyslexic children and normal readers were alike in that both were susceptible to lexical priming. All children made fewer errors when non-words were preceded by orthographically related real words than when they were presented in a neutral context. Our results were complicated by the fact that some of our reading age controls were at ceiling when reading non-words preceded by related primes, but the data did, at least, show that the context effect was operating normally for dyslexic readers. Their non-word reading improved by some 18.75 per cent when a priming context was provided; the corresponding benefit for normal readers was 8.75 per cent (see table 8.1).

Table 8.1 *Percentage of non-words read correctly by dyslexic readers and reading age matched controls, with and without orthographically related context*

	Neutral prime	Related prime	Context effect
Dyslexics	68.75	87.50	18.75
Reading age controls	85.00	93.75	8.75

Source: Snowling and Williams (unpublished)

To investigate the nature of the context effect, we examined the actual pronunciations of the non-word items. First we classified them as regular (e.g. *dreak* pronounced as 'dreek') or irregular (e.g. *dreak* pronounced as 'dreck'). The proportion of non-words pronounced in a regular way given the three different priming conditions is shown in table 8.2 where it can

Table 8.2 *Lexical influence on non-word decoding in dyslexic readers and reading age controls: proportion of pronunciations which were biased according to the preceding context*

Proportion of biased pronunciations	Nature of priming stimulus		
	Regular (moth)	Irregular (both)	Control (coth)
Dyslexics			
Regular	0.88	0.30	0.80
Irregular	0.05	0.56	0.08
Alternate	0.07	0.14	0.12
RA controls			
Regular	0.94	0.19	0.77
Irregular	0.03	0.72	0.15
Alternate	0.03	0.09	0.08

be compared with the proportion given an irregular or alternate pronunciation. Overall, dyslexic–normal differences were not significant but there were important differences between the context conditions. Non-words were most likely to be given a regular pronunciation when preceded by a regular or neutral prime. The proportion given such a pronunciation was dramatically reduced when the non-word was preceded by an irregular prime. The analysis of irregular pronunciations was complementary. A negligible number of non-words were given irregular pronunciations when preceded by regular or neutral primes but more than half of those preceded by irregular words were. As we only tested a small number of subjects, our results must be viewed as preliminary. However, they show that the reading of non-words by dyslexic children is subject to orthographic priming. A lexical influence can override the use of spelling-sound rules if testing conditions allow. Moreover, when non-words are presented in the context of real word stimuli, it may be possible to improve the performance of dyslexic readers to the level of reading age matched controls at least in so far as the reading of single syllable stimuli is concerned.

Fortunately, this conjecture would make sense of a recent failure to find non-word reading deficits in dyslexia (Treiman and Hirsh-Pasek 1985). In this experiment, 'component skills analysis' was used to compare a group of eleven-year-old dyslexic children reading at the eight- to nine-year level (grade level 2 to 3) with a group of normal readers matched for reading level. The children were asked to read 'triplets' containing regular, exception and nonsense words, all of similar orthographic structure (e.g. *bone/done/yone*; *days/says/tays*; *urchin/orchid/orchin*). The two groups were equated for performance on the regular word items which was a stringent matching procedure. When the groups were matched in this way, dyslexics read the irregular and nonsense words as well as the normal readers and they did not have any particular difficulty with the non-word items.

The authors consider a number of possible explanations for the discrepancy between their results and those of other studies. The non-words which they used, being all of one syllable, could have been too simple to pick up dyslexic-normal reader differences, or the training in phonic methods which their subjects had received may have accounted for their proficiency with spelling-sound rules (Snowling 1983). However, an alternative which they did not consider is that their experimental procedure may have induced orthographic priming. Put simply, a lexical context effect may have been operating to 'improve' the decoding skill of the dyslexics. Whereas *heaf* is normally pronounced by recourse to the rules h:/h/; *ea*:/i/; *f*/f/, when preceded by *deaf*, the analogy *eaf*:/ɛf/ was primed and the non-word produced after a two-step process rather than via the application of the usual three non-lexical rules. Of course, when dyslexics are presented with complex non-words which do not have lexical analogies, they are forced to resort to these rules and their deficit will be revealed (Snowling 1981).

Hence it seems possible for dyslexic readers to use orthographic context to compensate for their deficient decoding skill. Since an analogy strategy makes lesser demands on phoneme segmentation than does the use of grapheme-phoneme rules, this strategy will be especially preferred by individuals such as R.E. who have problems with the manipulation of phonemic information.

The use of context by dyslexic children

The idea that dyslexics might use alternative strategies in learning to read fits well within the interactive-compensatory framework proposed by Stanovich (1980). It will be recalled that Stanovich has argued that poor readers whose low-level decoding processes are slow make use of 'top-down' knowledge-based processes to compensate for their deficit. So, dyslexics may rely more heavily upon context during reading than do normal readers. Although we have concentrated primarily upon single-word decoding processes in this book, it must be remembered that most reading takes place in context. Dyslexics may therefore have a greater opportunity for learning words during their everyday reading experience than their phonological skills would predict. The way in which they might do this can be illustrated by one of the experiments we have already discussed (Frith and Snowling 1983, Experiment 5). In this experiment, dyslexic, normal and hyperlexic readers read a short passage comprising ten sentences. Each sentence contained a homograph – for example, 'They started to *row* across the river . . . She waved her wand and the boat became *minute*.' Subjects read the sentences aloud and the way in which they pronounced the homographs was recorded.

The three groups differed significantly from one another,

but the most interesting finding for present purposes was that the dyslexics actually did *better* than their Reading Age matched controls. They pronounced on average eight homographs correctly while normal readers managed only seven – a small but significant advantage that applied to all the dyslexic readers. These same dyslexics had done worse on a test of non-word reading than their controls. Yet, in spite of their decoding difficulty, they pronounced the homographs more accurately, suggesting that they were using context in a compensatory manner. Typically the dyslexics read more slowly than the other children and their behaviour on making an error was different. For instance when faced with the word *minute* in the above example, a difficult homograph for all the children, dyslexics stumbled over it, but many gave the response 'miniature'. Being semantically appropriate, this was an excellent substitution to make. In contrast, hyperlexics gave incorrect pronunciations and were quite unperturbed.

Thus, while hyperlexics seem to have an intact reading system without the usual links with cognitive and general knowledge systems, it could be that just such links allow dyslexics to read proficiently. Precisely how they might make use of semantic context during reading is suggested by the results of Pring and Snowling (1986). Recall that in this experiment it was found that pseudohomophonic non-words such as *nirse*, *wite*, were read more quickly by normal children if they were preceded by semantically related primes (*doctor–nirse*) than if they were preceded by a neutral context (*xxx–nirse*). The point to note here is that particular lexical entries can be primed via links with semantic memory. Non-words such as *peech* which are similar to primed real words (peach) can then be read via lexical means without resorting to phonological decoding processes. This would be similar to the process of reading by analogy envisaged in the case of R.E.

Take the non-word *nirse*. Having seen the word *doctor*, activation will automatically spread through the semantic memory network to related items such as *nurse*, *hospital* and *patient*. At least some of these items will have lexical representations within the reading system (depending upon the reading age of the subject in question). These lexical representations will receive activation and the printed words to which they correspond will subsequently be recognized more easily. In a sense the subject will be 'ready' to read the word *nurse* and we can infer that, if the non-word *nirse* were to be presented, this would be sufficiently similar to the expected item for the correct respone 'nurse' to be produced.

If dyslexics were capable of using the system just described, then this would afford them another means of reading novel words in the absence of grapheme-phoneme rules. Recently, in collaboration with Amanda Dooley, Linda Pring and I have been able to look at this possibility in a preliminary way. Using a paradigm similar to that of Pring and Snowling (1986), we tested twelve dyslexic children aged between nine and eleven years who were reading on average two years behind chronological age expectation. These were compared with a group of normal readers reading at the eight-year level (the reading age matched controls), and also a group of normal readers matched for chronological age, reading at the eleven year level. As before, subjects were presented with pseudohomophonic non-words to read and these were preceded by either related, unrelated or neutral primes.

First, we replicated our finding that non-word reading could be primed by a semantic context and, in line with the assumptions of Stanovich's model, less skilled readers (that is the dyslexics and their reading age controls) showed a larger context effect than the skilled eleven-year-old readers. The eleven-year-olds were in fact at ceiling on the test. Second, dyslexic children used context to at least the same extent as reading age matched controls (see figure 8.1). In fact they read the non-words some 400 milliseconds faster when they were preceded by related primes than when they were in a neutral context. Reading age controls benefited by a mere 100 milliseconds, but the difference was not statistically significant. So here is another way in which dyslexic children might learn to read even though their phonological skills are weak. The strategy proposed involves the use of intact semantic

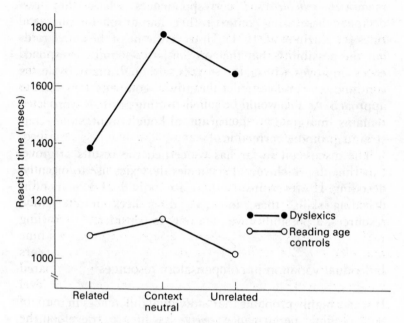

Figure 8.1. *The effects of semantically related and unrelated context on non-word reading in dyslexic readers and reading age matched controls*

processes which interact with, and prime, lexically-stored information. Stored orthographic information may facilitate the reading of novel words by lexical analogy. A further possibility is that stored auditory information, also activated, may speed the operation of phonetic decoding processes. In other words, the dyslexic children might begin to sound out a word even if tentatively, and the semantic information could enable them to complete the decoding process more quickly.

Hence, in the face of phonological difficulties, the reading development of dyslexic children may be fostered by the use of stored lexical and semantic information as well as by the use of more general knowledge resources. Moreover, because their visual processes are intact, and they find it easier to deal with whole-word than with segmental phonology, they might memorize *syllable-sound* correspondences where they can decipher these using context rather than grapheme-phoneme rules (cf. Rozin et al. 1971). However, none of the above rules out the possibility that their use of letter-sound correspondences improves with age – it does, although many dyslexics continue to prefer an alternative, compensatory visual approach. As a consequence, their reading at single word level remains marginally inaccurate although contextual constraints promote correction.

The discussion so far has concerned the results of group experiments which reveal strategies dyslexics use to promote decoding. However, just as there are individual differences in decoding skills, there must be differences in alternative resources, a possibility we turn now to consider.

Individual variation in compensatory resources

It seems highly probable that individual differences in reading and spelling performance *emerge* as literacy development proceeds. One viable hypothesis is that children who have good visual memory resources rely upon orthographic strategies for reading, abstracting higher-order rules or analogies on the basis of the printed words they already know. A second is that children whose language resources are good, especially if their verbal I.Q. is high, rely heavily upon semantic memory processes to foster their reading development.

Interestingly, Olson and his colleagues have come to broadly similar conclusions and looked into the possibility using a multivariate approach. Olson et al. (1985) administered a number of different tests of phonological and orthographic processing to groups of dyslexic and normal readers. Their findings will come as no surprise; the dyslexics were uniquely deficient in phonological coding. They made more errors than controls on a rhyming test involving non-words – that is, they found it more difficult to decide whether or not *caik* and *dake* rhymed. Their oral non-word reading was also poorer than that of controls. However, the two groups did not differ in their use of phonological coding for lexical access, and both showed the regularity effect. Olson's explanation for this is illuminating and it deserves discussion here.

Olson et al. found that, after controlling for reading age, differences in the regular word advantage correlated not with phonological ability, but with orthographic skill. Seemingly, orthographic skill reduced the size of the regularity effect by *decreasing* the errors on irregular words. Thus, for the children they tested, an advantage for regular words only signalled the use of a phonological strategy when orthographic skill was weak. This is quite different from the claims made by other authors who assume that a knowledge of grapheme-phoneme rules makes regular words easier to read than irregular items. Moreover, Olson and his colleagues went on to suggest that a single dimension of orthographic skill could account for different surface manifestations of dyslexia. Children with weak orthographic images make most use of phonological codes in lexical access and they also use phonological skills in spelling. On the other hand, children with strong orthographic images who show a reduced regularity effect tend to make non-phonetic spelling errors.

Olson et al. are making a point similar to the one developed in this book but on different grounds. The basic tenet is that dyslexics are subject to a phonological deficit which renders them slow to acquire phonological codes. However, these codes do emerge and they may slowly develop but, over and above them, compensatory strategies are laid down. To a large extent it is these compensatory strategies which dictate individual differences in reading and spelling skill. Olson et al. took the argument a step further by monitoring the eye-movements which the dyslexics made during prose reading. An important dimension of reading style emerged. At one pole, a small number of children were 'plodders' .These children read from word to word with a high proportion of regressive movements. At the other end, an equivalent number were 'explorers', that is children who read with a higher proportion of forward movements, skipping words. The majority of the sample fell between the two extremes. Thus Olson et al. argued that this dimension of reading style was normally distributed, and it turned out that an individual's position on the dimension was preditable from other of their cognitive characteristics: for younger subjects, orthographic skill predicted where they would fall in the plodder–explorer dimension. Children with weak orthographic images (those who used phonology more) tended to be 'plodders' whereas the 'explorers' were children with stronger orthographic images. For older subjects it was Verbal I.Q. which predicted reading style: children with higher verbal skills were the 'explorers' while children with poorer language skills fell towards the 'plodder' end of the dimension. Here Olson and his colleagues ran into the familiar 'chicken-or-egg' problem. Was it that Verbal I.Q. induced an explorer-reading style conducive to the development of orthographic images or was it that children with weak phonological skill became explorers as a way of handling their basic decoding deficiency? The only lead we have is the evidence from hyperlexia. In this work, Verbal I.Q. predicted comprehension skill and, presumably, a more 'exploratory' approach to printed materials.

Olson et al. summarize their own particular view in the following way: 'the correlations suggest an interaction between basic phonological coding skills and higher level verbal skills in determining subjects' ability to recognize words. The more verbally intelligent can supplement their weak phonological skills and can reach a level which the less verbally intelligent would have to use phonological skills to reach'. The validity of their hypothesis remains to be seen, but it is worth pursuing.

How do dyslexics learn to spell?

Finally, a brief word about spelling. Spelling is a more difficult process than reading – it involves retrieval rather than recognition processes and, to quote Frith and Frith (1980), whereas reading can proceed on the basis of 'partial cues', spelling requires full information. The idea we have been considering with regard to the development of reading processes is that dyslexics rely heavily upon context to promote their decoding skill. This will have least two implications for the development of spelling.

Assuming a phonological basis to the dyslexics' deficit, the alphabetic strategy is, by definition, difficult for them. More importantly, reliance upon context and a reading style after the fashion of an 'explorer', is not conducive to the develop-ment of the detailed orthographic representations which are required for accurate spelling in a language such as English. Moreover, while context fulfils a monitoring function during reading, the only way to check spelling accuracy is by reference to an internal representation. Dyslexics do not normally possess these representations.

So dyslexics fare much less well in spelling than they do in reading. Those who violate this rule and spell well probably acquire the skill through explicit learning. Many dyslexics memorize spellings according to letter names. R.E. did this to some extent. Others have their attention specifically drawn to spelling patterns and conventions through multisensory teaching and Bradley (1981) describes *simultaneous oral spelling*, an effective remedial technique in which spellings are learned by recitation of letter names in combination with writing. Without these or similar compensatory devices such as the use of mnemonics, the spelling of dyslexic children remains at best phonetic, at worst, indecipherable. In the latter case, the insightful dyslexic is likely to avoid writing altogether, although he or she may enjoy reading by virtue of visually-based strategies.

There are, then, a number of ways in which the literacy development of dyslexic children could take a different course from that followed by normal reader/spellers. To an extent, a similar end-point will be reached, although persisting deficits will be detectable if sufficiently subtle tests are applied. It would be naive to think that every dyslexic child compensates in the same way – individual resources will differ as will motivation to succeed. It will be necessary to take account of all these factors, cognitive and temperamental, if we are to arrive at a satisfactory definition of dyslexia.

Synthesis: towards a definition of dyslexia

The evidence presented within this chapter makes clear that dyslexia is a disorder with a number of different manifestations. There is no doubt that children who have unexpected problems with literacy exist but the task of describing them is fraught. First, dyslexia is a developmental disorder; its nature changes with time. Second, when setting up criteria which distinguish dyslexic from normal readers, it is necessary to take account of their strengths, about which we know little, as well as their deficits, about which we know more. So far, 'dyslexia' has defied definition.

Nonetheless, the cognitive-developmental perspective is useful. It grew from the experimental work on groups of dyslexics which set them apart from normal readers. However, it can also accommodate the results of single case studies which reveal individual differences between dyslexic children. The predominant view to date is that dyslexia is associated with phonological difficulties originating within spoken language processes. Since phoneme segmentation skill is required to develop literacy within an alphabetic writing system, a child who does not possess this ability at the critical time will fail to learn to read and spell. However, prolonged failure is not inevitable and development can proceed. Its course will depend upon a number of interacting factors and these form the basis of a new hypothesis.

The main proposal is that prognosis depends primarily upon the extent of the child's phonological disorder, that is its severity. But this is not the only predictor. The other processes which contribute towards literacy development, namely visual, lexical and semantic resources, are crucial as is the teaching the child receives. Furthermore, progress will be tempered by motivational factors.

The first prediction is that there is a subgroup of dyslexic children who are developmentally delayed. The delay may be genetic, environmental or even emotional in origin. These children are not 'ready' to read at the expected time within the present educational system, but their phonological difficulties are mild. So it is possible that with maturity they will gradually develop along normal lines and be indistinguishable from reading age matched controls. However, this can only be the case if there is no disparity between visual-perceptual, semantic and phonological skills. If there is, and perceptual or semantic skills are the stronger, then atypical development will be precipitated. The child will not await phonological development but will start to read using compensatory visual strategies guided by contextual cues. The result will be a classic dyslexic profile; non-word reading will be poor and spelling dysphonetic unless, of course, phonic teaching has been stressed.

The second prediction is that there is a subgroup of children who have specific phonological deficits. Their difficulties, which can be severe, are probably due to underlying language disabilities. Maturation will not resolve their problems in auditory-verbal processing, so they will not be able to use phonological strategies for reading or spelling. Prognosis will depend upon how intact alternative cognitive resources are, although teaching will play a role.

It is important to point out that the distinction made here between the different modes of development is not simply a distinction between developmental 'lag' and developmental 'disorder'. Rather the distinction between delay and disorder has been made with reference to the skills which underlie reading and spelling, particularly language skills. A delay in the acquisition of prerequisite skills can precipitate *either* a delay *or* a disorder of literacy, depending upon the integrity of compensatory resources. A disorder, on the other hand, always leads to an atypical pattern of reading and spelling.

If the hypothesis is correct then it will allow us to account for the different patterns of reading and spelling style which have been attributed to dyslexic individuals. The dyseidetic or surface dyslexic profile, characterized by phonological reading and phonetic spelling, will be associated with delayed reading development along normal lines, especially where visual or semantic skills are weak. The dysphonetic or phonological dyslexic profile will be associated with delayed phonological development where visual or semantic skills are strong, or with disordered phonological development.

How should we teach dyslexic children?

The present proposals have fairly direct practical implications. Since the primary factor dictating progress is phonological skill then early intervention to promote this vital resource is an obvious necessity. There is already evidence from the studies of Bradley and Bryant (1983) that training in sound categorization can assist reading and spelling development. In their longitudinal study, they identified children 'at risk' of reading and spelling problems at four to five years of age, before they had started to read. They did this by reading out to the children three or four words and the children had to say which of the words did not rhyme with the others, or which one started with a different sound. Children who had difficulty with these tests of rhyme and alliteration were destined to be poorer readers than other children who could easily complete the segmentation task.

A subset of the 'at risk' group were chosen for training in sound categorization. They were seen for weekly individual sessions over two school years and were taught to categorize pictures according to the shared sound similarity of their names. For instance, the children learned to place *hat* and *cat* together because they rhyme, and later on they learned to place *hat* with *hen* because the two names begin with the same sound. A second group of 'at risk' children were seen individually for the same amount of time. They worked with identical cards to the sound-training group, but instead they learned to sort the cards into semantic categories. For instance, they would place *pig* and *dog* together, as they are both animals and later, to place *dog* with *cat* as they are both domestic animals.

Four years after the start of the project, when the children were eight years old, they were retested. The results were significant. Firstly, children who had been given training had progressed further than a no-intervention control group. More importantly, children who had received sound training did better in both reading and spelling than the group trained to work with semantic categories. This was true even when the substantial effects of I.Q. and social class were removed by a statistical technique. Furthermore, the effect of sound training was specific to the acquisition of written language skills. It had no differential effect on performance in mathematics. We can conclude from this study that early training in sound categorization has a beneficial effect on the acquisition of reading and spelling skills. We do not know whether children with persisting phonological problems also benefit from this type of intervention although teachers and therapists who work with older dyslexics suggest they do. Bradley and Bryant's study concentrated upon promoting a weak skill – namely sound categorisation. This should place the child in a better position for acquiring alphabetic skills. An alternative approach is to directly to enhance the child's ability to deal with printed words: that is, explicitly to show the child orthographic patterns so that the phonological analysis which usually makes it possible to abstract them will not be required.

What I shall say here is speculative but essentially it follows the lead set by dyslexics themselves in learning to read. It looks at the use of lexical units larger than the grapheme-phoneme correspondence (lexical analogies) for reading and spelling. The basic requirements of this approach are a knowledge of single letter-sound correspondences, and the ability to segment spoken words into the units of onset and rime (c–oat, l–ake). We have seen that this subsyllabic segmentation process places fewer demands on phonological processes than phoneme parsing and therefore it is more likely to be within the reach of 'classically' dyslexic children.

So, with these two necessary skills at the ready, the child might be shown a 'family' of words, say *rain, pain, stain, drain.* By placing these together, and perhaps using plastic letters, the shared letter string *ain* is explicit. It forms a cohesive unit which is usually pronounced [εIn]. The child can learn this orthographic pattern and its corresponding sound and need not discover it for him or herself. Moreover, access to this lexical analogy will provide the child with a means of reading novel words and of writing unfamiliar spellings which contain the sound component [εIn].

Many teachers probably already use this technique to an extent. However, it is rather different from the strategy advocated by the structured multisensory methods such as Orton-Gillingham-Stillman that have been successful with dyslexic children. These methods systematically teach the child grapheme-phoneme rules, for example 'ai' for [εI], 'ea' for [i], as a foundation for literacy. There are some advantages of the present method over these rule learning techniques; in reading, it reduces the sound blending which is required – fewer units have to be put together to build 'rain' from 'r-ain' than from 'r-ai-n'; in spelling it reduces the load on auditory memory in that fewer sound units need to be held during the transcription process.

Interestingly, Goswami (1986) has reported that beginning readers can make use of such lexical 'analogies' in their reading to positive effect. She gave young readers a clue-word, for example *beak*, telling them its pronunciation and that it could help them to read some other words. She then presented words like *peak* and *weak*. The children, who were still relative novices, then read these target words better than if the clue words shared letters with targets but were not analogous to them, as where *beak* was the clue for *bask*. Since Goswami's readers were presumably within the logographic phase, there is every reason to suppose that dyslexics who are failing to cross the alphabetic 'barrier' will also be able to make effective use of this strategy.

I do not wish in any way to dismiss the traditional teaching methods advocated by Orton-Gillingham-Stillman which focus upon teaching rules. These methods are well tried and tested, if not researched. They are certainly effective, but we need to know why. An important feature of them is that they are multisensory. When a new spelling pattern is introduced, the child sees it, says it, writes it, feels it. Hulme (1981), who recommends multisensory teaching, has shown in a series of experiments that disabled readers remember letter-strings better if they are allowed to trace them. The beneficial effect of tracing was greater for poor readers than for normal readers who already had efficient (phonological) memory codes at their disposal. So it is good practice to encourage dyslexics to use *all* their senses during learning – to rely upon their strengths to compensate for and circumvent their weaknesses.

Strangely, the literature on dyslexia has focused more upon its associated factors than upon its remediation. The way forward is to investigate how individual dyslexic children with individual patterns of cognitive ability respond to different teaching techniques. We must find out how the nature and the rate of their learning differs from that of normally developing children and how the manifestation of dyslexia changes as time proceeds. Only then we will have the certain knowledge of how to teach dyslexic children.

Epilogue

In this book we have progressed from a medical definition of dyslexia which is difficult to put into practice, through a statistical definition which defines unexpected reading failure by the 'discrepancy' principle. Dissatisfaction with both positions led us to consider the cognitive deficits of children with specific reading difficulties within a developmental framework.

So what have we learned? The prevalent view from studies examining groups of 'dyslexic' children is that they have specific problems with verbal memory, verbal labelling and other aspects of auditory processing. They do not have the phonological skills required to learn to read at the *critical* time. For many dyslexics, this brings about failure to progress to the alphabetic phase of literacy development: they are unable to tackle unfamiliar words in their reading and their spelling is dysphonetic. We still need to know more about individual dyslexics and how they compare with normally developing readers of the same reading age; how those who are different from the above and possess alphabetic reading and spelling skills differ cognitively from those who do not. We also need to know if the teaching they have been given has promoted their alphabetic competence.

So where do we stand? Questions remain about how the cognitive characteristics of individual dyslexic children interact with the demands of learning to read. It will only be possible to discover the answers by looking at the ways in which these children respond to different teaching techniques, and by following their progress over time.

References

Atkinson, R. C. and Shiffrin, R. M. (1968): Human memory: a proposed system and its control processes. In Spence, K. W. and Spence J. T. (eds), *The Psychology of Learning and Motivation: advances in research and theory* 2. New York: Academic Press.

Backman, J. E., Mamen, M. and Ferguson, H. B. (1984): Reading level design: conceptual and methodological issues in reading research. *Psychological Bulletin*, 96, 560–8.

Baddeley, A., Ellis, N., Miles, T. and Lewis, V. (1982): Developmental and acquired dyslexia: a comparison. *Cognition*, 11, 185–99.

Baron, J. and Strawson, C. (1976): Use of orthographic and word-specific knowledge in reading words aloud. *Journal of Experimental Psychology: Human Perception and Performance*, 2, 386–93.

Baron, J. and Treiman, R. (1980): Some problems in the study of differences in cognitive processes. *Memory and Cognition*, 8, 313–21.

Baron J., Treiman, R., Wilf, J. F. and Kellman, P. (1980): Spelling and reading by rules. In Frith, U. (ed.), *Cognitive Processes in Spelling*. London: Academic Press.

Barron, R. W. (1980): Visual and phonological strategies in reading and spelling. In U. Frith (ed.), *Cognitive Processes in Spelling*. London: Academic Press.

Bauer, R. H. and Emhert, J. (1984): Information processing in reading disabled and nondisabled readers. *Journal of Experimental Child Psychology*, 37, 271–81.

Bishop, D. V. M. (1982): *T.R.O.G. Test for Reception of Grammar*. Abingdon, Oxon.: Thomas Leach Ltd.

Bishop, D. V. M. (1985): Spelling ability in congenital dysarthria: evidence against articulatory coding in translating between phonemes and graphemes. *Cognitive Neuuropsychology*, 2, 229–51.

Bissex, G. L. (1980): *GNYS at Work: a child learns to write and read*. Cambridge, MA: Harvard University Press.

Boder, E. (1971): Developmental dyslexia: prevailing diagnostic concepts. In Myklebust, J.(ed.), *Progress in Learning Disabilities*. New York: Grune and Stratton.

Boder, E. (1973): Developmental dyslexia: a diagnostic approach based on three atypical reading-spelling patterns. *Developmental Medicine and Child Neurology*, 15, 663–87.

Bradley, L. (1980): *Assessing Reading Difficulties*. London: Macmillan Educational.

Bradley, L. and Bryant, P. (1978): Difficulties in auditory organisation as a possible cause of reading backwardness. *Nature*, 271, 746–7.

Bradley, L. and Bryant, P. (1979): Independence of reading and spelling in backward and normal readers. *Developmental Medicine and Child Neurology*, 21, 504–14.

Bradley, L. and Bryant, P. (1983): Categorising sounds and learning to read: a causal connexion. *Nature*, 301, 419.

Brady, S., Shankweiler, D. and Mann, V. (1983): Speech perception and memory coding in relation to reading ability. *Journal of Experimental Psychology*, 35, 345–67.

Brandt, J. and Rosen, J. J. (1980): Auditory-phonemic perception in dyslexia: categorised identification and discrimination of stop consonants. *Brain and Language*, 9, 324–37.

Bryant, P. and Impey, L. (1986): The similarities between normal readers and developmental and acquired dyslexics. *Cognition*, 24, 121–37.

Byrne, B. and Shea, P. (1979): Semantic and phonetic memory codes in beginning readers. *Memory and Cognition*, 7, 333–8.

Carr, T. H. (1985): *The Development of Reading Skills*. San Francisco: Jossey-Bass.

Campbell, R. (1985): When children write non-words to dictation. *Journal of Experimental Child Psychology*, 40, 133–51.

Campbell, R. and Butterworth, B. (1985): Phonological dyslexia and dysgraphia in a highly literate subject; a developmental case with associated deficits of phonemic awareness and processing. *Quarterly Journal of Experimental Psychology*, 37A, 435–75.

Cobrinik, L. (1982): The performance of hyperlexic children on an 'incomplete words' task. *Neuropsychologia*, 20, 569–77.

Cohen, R. L. and Netley, C. (1981): Short term memory deficits in reading-disabled children in the absence of opportunity for rehearsal strategies. *Intelligence*, 5, 69–76.

Coltheart, M. (1980): Analysing reading disorders. Unpublished clinical tests, Birkbeck College, University of London.

Coltheart, M. Patterson, K. and Marshall, J. C. (1980): *Deep Dyslexia*. London: Routledge and Kegan Paul.

Coltheart, M., Masterson, J., Byng, S., Prior, M. and Riddoch, J. (1983): Surface dyslexia. *Quarterly Journal of Experimental Psychology*, 35A, 469–96.

Conrad, R. (1964): Acoustic confusions in immediate memory. *British Journal of Psychology*, 55, 75–84.

Craik, F. I. M. and Lockhart, R. S. (1972): Levels of processing: a framework for memory research. *Journal of Verbal Learning and Verbal Behaviour*, 11, 671–84.

Crary, M. A. (1984): A neurolinguistic perspective on developmental verbal dyspraxia. *Communicative Disorders*, 9, 33–49.

Critchley, M. (1970): *The Dyslexic Child*. London: Heinemann Medical Books.

Critchley, M. and Critchley, E. A. (1978): *Dyslexia Defined*. London: Acford.

Denckla, M. B. and Rudel, R. G. (1976a): Naming of object drawings by dyslexic and other learning-disabled children. *Brain and Language*, 3, 1–15.

Denckla, M. and Rudel, R. (1976b): Rapid automatised naming: dyslexia differentiated from other learning disabilities. *Neuropsychologia*, 14, 471–9.

Dunn, L. M. (1982): *The British Picture Vocabulary Scale*. Windsor: NFER-Nelson.

Ehri, L. (1985): Sources of difficulty in learning to spell and read. In Wolraich, M. L. and Routh, D. (eds), *Advances in Developmental and Behavioural Paediatrics*. Greenwich, Conn.: Jai Press Inc.

Ehri, L. C. and Wilce, L. S. (1980): The influence of orthography on readers' conceptualisation of the phonemic structure of words. *Applied Psycholinguistics*, 1, 371–85.

Elliott, D. E. and Needleman, R. M. (1976): The syndrome of hyperlexia. *Brain and Language*, 3, 339–49.

Ellis, A. W. (1979): Developmental and acquired dyslexia: some observations on Jorm (1979). *Cognition*, 7, 413–20.

Ellis, A. W (1982): Spelling and writing (and reading and speaking). In Ellis, A. W. (ed.), *Normality and Pathology in Cognitive Functions*. London: Academic Press.

Ellis, A. W. (1984): *Reading, Writing and Dyslexia*. London: Lawrence Erlbaum Ass.

Ellis, A. W. (1985): The cognitive neuropsychology of developmental (and acquired) dyslexia: a critical survey. *Cognitive Neuropsychology*, 2, 169–205.

Ellis, N. (1981): Visual and name coding in dyslexic children. *Psychological Research*, 43, 201–18.

Ellis, N. C. and Miles, T. R. (1981): A lexical encoding deficiency II. In Pavlidis, G. Th. and Miles, T. R. (eds), *Dyslexia Research and its Applications to Education*. Cambridge, Mass.: MIT Press.

Farnham-Diggory, S. and Nelson, B. (1983): Microethology of spelling behaviours in normal and dyslexic development. In Rogers, D. A. and Sloboda, J. A. (eds), *The Acquisition of Symbolic Skills*. New York: Plenum Press.

Frith, U. (1978): Spelling difficulties. *Journal of Child Psychology and Child Psychiatry*, 19, 279–85.

Frith, U. (1979): Reading by eye and writing by ear. In Bouma, H., Kolers, P. A. and Wrolstad, M. E. (eds), *The Processing of Visible Language*. New York: Plenum Press.

Frith, U. (1980): Unexpected spelling problems. In Frith, U. (ed.), *Cognitive Processes in Spelling*. London: Academic Press.

Frith, U. (1981): Experimental approaches to developmental dyslexia: an introduction. *Psychological Research*, 43, 97–109.

Frith, U. (1984): Specific spelling problems. In Malatesha, R. N. and Whitaker, H. A. (eds), *Dyslexia: A Global Issue*. The Hague: Martinus Nijhoff.

Frith, U. (1985): Beneath the surface of developmental dyslexia. In Patterson, K. E., Marshall, J. C. and Coltheart, M. (eds), *Surface Dyslexia*. London: Routledge and Kegan Paul.

Frith, U. and Frith, C.D. (1980): Relationships between reading and spelling. In Kavanagh, J. F. and Venezky, R. L. (eds), *Orthography, Reading and Dyslexia*. Baltimore: University Park Press.

Frith, U. and Snowling, M. (1983): Reading for meaning and reading for sound in autistic and dyslexic children. *British Journal of Developmental Psychology*, 1, 329–42.

Funnell, E. (1983): Phonological processes in reading: new evidence from acquired dyslexia. *British Journal of Psychology*, 74, 159–80.

Glushko, R. J. (1979): The organization and activation of orthographic knowledge in reading aloud. *Journal of Experimental Psychology: Human Perception and Performance*, 5, 674–91.

Godfrey, J. J., Syrdal-Lasky, A. K., Millay, K. K. and Knox, C. M. (1981): Performance of dyslexic children on speech perception test. *Journal of Experimental Child Psychology*, 32, 401–24.

Goldberg, T. E. and Rothermel, R. D. (1984): Hyperlexic children reading. *Brain*, 107, 759–85.

Goodglass, H. and Kaplan, E. (1983): *Assessment of aphasia and related disorders* Philadelphia: Lea and Febiger.

Goodman, K. S. (1973): Psycholinguistic universals in the reading process. In Smith, F., *Psycholinguistics and Reading*. New York: Holt, Rinehart and Winston.

Goswami, U. (1986): Children's use of analogy in learning to read: a developmental study. *Journal of Experimental Child Psychology*, 42, 73–83.

Gough, P. and Hillinger, M. L. (1980): Learning to read: an unnatural act. *Bulletin of the Orton Society*, 30, 179–96.

Goyen, J. D. and Martin, M. (1977): The relation of spelling errors to cognitive variables and word type. *British Journal of Psychology*, 47, 268–73.

Hall, J. W., Ewing, A., Tinzmann, M. B. and Wilson, K. P. (1981): Phonetic coding in dyslexic and normal readers. *Bulletin of the Psychonomic Society*, 17, 177–8.

Healy, J. M. (1982): The enigma of hyperlexia. *Reading Research Quarterly*, 7, 319–38.

Healy, J. M., Aram, D. M., Horowitz, S. J. and Kessler, J. W. (1982): A study of hyperlexia. *Brain and Language*, 17, 1–23.

Hermelin, B. and O'Connor, N. (1970): *Psychological experiments with autistic children*. Oxford: Pergamon Press.

Holmes, J. M. (1978): 'Regression' and reading breakdown. In Caramzza, A. and Zurif, E. B. (eds), *Language Acquisition and Language Breakdown: parallels and divergences*. Baltimore: Johns Hopkins Press.

Holmes, D. L. and Pepper, R. J. (1977): An evaluation of the use of spelling error analysis in the diagnosis of reading disabilities. *Child Development*, 48, 1708–11.

Hulme, C. (1981): *Reading Retardation and Multisensory Learning*. London: Routledge and Kegan Paul.

Hulme, C., Sylvester, J., Smith, S. and Muir, C. (1986): The effects of word length on memory for pictures: evidence for speech coding in young children. *Journal of Experimental Child Psychology*, 41, 61–75.

Huttenlocher, P. and Huttenlocher, J. (1973): A study of children with hyperlexia. *Neurology*, 23, 1107–16.

Johnston, R. S. (1982): Phonological coding in dyslexic readers. *British Journal of Psychology*, 73, 455–60.

Johnston, R. S. (1983): Developmental deep dyslexia? *Cortex*, 19, 133–9.

Jorm, A. F. (1979): The cognitive and neurological basis of developmental dyslexia: a theoretical framework and review. *Cognition*, 7, 19–33.

Jorm, A. F. (1981): Children with reading and spelling retardation: Functioning of whole-word and correspondence-rule mechanisms. *Journal of Child Psychology and Psychiatry*, 22, 171–8.

Jorm, A. F. and Share, D. L. (1983): Phonological reading and reading acquisition. *Applied Psycholinguistics*, 4, 103–47.

Katz, R. B. (1986): Phonological deficiencies in children with reading disability: evidence from an object naming test. *Cognition*, 22, 225–57.

Kay, J. and Marcel, T. (1981): One process not two in reading aloud: lexical analogies do the work of non-lexical rules. *Quarterly Journal of Experimental Psychology*, 33A, 397–413.

Klein, G. S. (1964): Semantic power measured through the interference of words with colour naming. *American Journal of Psychology*, 77, 576–88.

Klein, H. (1985): The assessment of some persisting language difficulties in the learning disabled. In Snowling, M. J. (ed.), *Children's Written Language Difficulties*. Windsor: NFER-Nelson.

Kochnower, J., Richardson, E. and DiBenedetto, B. (1983): A comparison of the phonic decoding ability of normal and learning disabled children. *Journal of Learning Disabilities*, 16, 348–51.

La Berge, D. and Samuels, S. J. (1974): Toward a theory of automatic information processing in reading. *Cognitive Psychology*, 6, 293–323.

Liberman, I. Y. and Shankweiler, D. (1979): Speech, the alphabet and teaching to read. In Resnick, L. and Weaver, P. (eds), *Theory and Practice of Early Reading*. Hillsdale, N.J.: Lawrence Erlbaum Ass.

Liberman, I. Y., Shankweiler, D., Liberman, A., Fowler, C. and Fischer, F.W. (1977): Phonetic segmentation and recoding in the beginning reader. In Reber, A. S. and Scarborough, D. L. (eds), *Towards a Psychology of Reading*. Lawrence Erlbaum Ass.

Mann, V. A., Liberman, I. Y. and Shankweiler, D. (1980): Children's memory for sentences and word strings in relation to reading ability. *Memory and Cognition*, 8, 329–35.

Marcel, T. (1980a): Phonological awareness and phonological representation: investigation of a specific spelling problem. In Frith, U. (ed.), *Cognitive Processes in Spelling*. London: Academic Press.

Marcel, T. (1980b): Surface dyslexia and beginning reading : a revised hypothesis of the pronunciation of print and its impairments. In Coltheart, M., Patterson, K. E. and Marshall, J. C. (eds), *Deep Dyslexia*. London : Routledge and Kegan Paul.

Mark, L.S., Shankweiler, D., Liberman, I. Y. and Fowler, C. A. (1977): Phonetic recoding and reading difficulty in beginning readers. *Memory and Cognition*, 5, 623–9.

Marsh, G. and Desberg, P. (1983): The development of strategies in the acquisition of symbolic skills. In Rogers, D. A. and Sloboda, J. A. (eds), *The Acquisition of Symbolic Skills*. New York: Plenum Press.

Marsh, G., Friedman, M., Welch, V. and Desberg, P. (1980): The development of strategies in spelling. In Frith, U., (ed.), *Cognitive Processes in Spelling*. London: Academic Press.

Marsh, G., Friedman, M., Welch, V. and Desberg, P. (1981): A cognitive–developmental theory of reading acquisition. *Reading Research: advances in theory and practice*, 3. New York: Academic Press.

Marshall, J. C. (1984): Toward a rational taxonomy of the developmental dyslexias. In Malatesha, R. N. and Whitaker, H. A. (eds), *Dyslexia: a global issue*. The Hague: Martinus Nijhoff.

Masterson, J. (1985): On how we read nonwords – data from different populations. In Patterson, K. E., Marshall, J. C. and Coltheart, M. (eds), *Surface Dyslexia. Neuropsychological and Cognitive studies of Phonological Reading*. London: Routledge and Kegan Paul.

Mehegan, C. and Dreyfuss, F. (1972): Hyperlexia. *Neurology*, 22, 1105–11.

Miles, T. R. (1983): *Dyslexia: the pattern of difficulties*. London: Granada.

Mitterer, J. O. (1982): There are at least two kinds of poor readers: whole-word poor readers and recoding poor readers. *Canadian Journal of Psychology*, 36, 445–61.

Morais, J., Cary, L., Alegria, J. and Bertelson, P. (1979): Does awareness of speech as a sequence of phones arise spontaneously? *Cognition*, 7, 323–31.

Morrison, F. J. (1984): Reading disability: a problem in rule learning and word decoding. *Developmental Review*, 4, 36–47.

Morrison, F. J. and Manis, F.R. (1982): Cognitive processes in reading disability: a critique and proposal. In Brainerd, C. J. and Pressley, M. (eds), *Progress in Cognitive Development Research*. New York: Springer-Verlag.

Morton, J. (1969): Interaction of information in word recognition. *Psychological Review*, 76, 165–78.

Naidoo, S. (1972): *Specific Dyslexia*. London: Pitman Publishing.

Neely, J.H. (1977): Semantic priming and retrieval from lexical memory: roles of inhibitionless spreading activation and limited capacity attention. *Journal of Experimental Psychology: General*, 106, 226–54.

Nelson, H. E. (1980): Analysis of spelling errors in normal and dyslexic children. In Frith, U. (ed.), *Cognitive Processes in Spelling*. London: Academic Press.

Nelson, H. and Warrington, E. K. (1974): Developmental spelling retardation and its relation to other cognitive abilities. *British Journal of Psychology*, 65, 265–74.

Olson, R. K., Kliegel, R., Davidson, B. J. and Davies, S. E. (1984): Development of phonetic memory in disabled and normal readers. *Journal of Experimental Child Psychology*, 37, 187–206.

Olson, R. K., Kliegel, R., Davidson, B. J. and Foltz, G. (1985): Individual and developmental differences in reading disability. In Waller, T. G. (ed.), *Reading Research: advances in theory and practice: 4*. New York: Academic Press.

Orton, S. T. (1925): 'Word blindness' in school children. *Archives of Neurology and Psychiatry*, 14, 581–615.

Patterson, K. E., Marshall, J. C. and Coltheart, M. (eds), (1985): *Surface Dyslexia: neuropsychological and cognitive studies of phonological reading*. London: Lawrence Erlbaum Ass.

Perfetti, C. A., Goldman, S. R. and Hogaboam, T. W. (1979): Reading skill and the identification of words in discourse context. *Memory and Cognition*, 7, 273–82.

Perfetti, C. A. and Hogaboam, T. (1975): The relationship between simple word decoding and reading comprehension skill. *Journal of Educational Psychology*, 67, 461–9.

Perfetti, C. A. and McCutchen, D. (1982): Speech processes in reading. In Lass, N. J. (ed.), *Speech and Language: advances in basic research and practice*, 6. London: Academic Press.

Perfetti, C. A. and Roth, S. (1981): Some of the interactive processes in reading and their role in reading skill. In Lesgold, A. M. and Perfetti, C. A. (eds), *Interactive Processes in Reading*. Hillsdale, N.J.: Lawrence Erlbaum Ass.

Perin, D. (1981): Spelling, reading and adult literacy. *Psychological Research*, 43, 245–57.

Perin, D. (1983): Phonemic segmentation and spelling. *British Journal of Psychology*, 74, 129–44.

Posner, M. I. and Snyder, C. R. R. (1975): Attention and cognitive control. In Solso, R. L (ed.), *Information Processing and Cognition. The Loyola Symposium*. Hillsdale, N.J.: Lawrence Erlbaum Ass.

Pring, L. and Snowling, M. (1986): Developmental changes in word recognition: an information processing account. *Quarterly Journal of Experimental Psychology*, 38A, 395–418.

Prior, M. and McCorriston, M. (1984): Acquired and developmental spelling dyslexia. *Brain and Language*, 20, 263–85.

Rack, J. (1985): Orthographic and phonetic encoding in normal and dyslexic readers. *British Journal of Psychology*, 76, 325–40.

Read, C. (1971): Preschool children's knowledge of English phonology. *Harvard Educational Review*, 41, 1–34.

Read, C. (1975): Lessons to be learned from the preschool orthographer. In Lennenberg, E. H. and Lennenberg, E. (eds), *Foundations of Language Development*, 2. London: Academic Press.

Read, C. (1986): *Children's Creative Spelling*. London: Routledge and Kegan Paul.

Robinson, P., Beresford, R. and Dodd, B. (1982): Spelling errors made by speech disordered children. *Spelling Progress Bulletin*, 22, 19–20.

Rodgers, B. (1983): The identification and prevalence of specific reading retardation. *British Journal of Educational Psychology*, 53, 369–73.

Rourke, B. P. (1983): Reading and spelling disabilities: a developmental neuropsychological perspective. In Kirk, U. (ed.), *Neuropsychology of Language, Reading and Spelling*. New York: Academic Press.

Rozin, P. and Gleitman, L. (1977): The structure and acquisition of reading II: the reading process and the acquisition of the alphabetic principle. In Reber, A. S. and Scarborough, D. L. (eds), *Towards a Psychology of Reading*. Hillsdale, NJ: Lawrence Erlbaum Ass.

Rozin, P., Poritsky, S. and Sotsky, R. (1971): American children with reading problems can easily learn to read English represented by Chinese characters. *Science*, 171, 1264–7.

Rutter, M. and Yule, W. (1975): The concept of specific reading retardation. *Journal of Child Psychology and Psychiatry*, 16, 181–97.

Rutter, M., Tizard, J. and Whitmore, K. (eds) (1970): *Education, Health and Behaviour*. London: Longmans.

Schwantes, F. M. (1981): Locus of the context effect in children's word recognition. *Child Development*, 52, 895–903.

Schwantes, F. M. (1985): Expectancy integration and interactional processes: age differences in the nature of words affected by sentence context. *Journal of Experimental Child Psychology*, 31, 212–29.

Seidenberg, M. S. and Tanenhaus, M. K. (1979): Orthographic effects on rhyme monitoring. *Journal of Experimental Psychology: Human Learning and Memory*, 5, 546–54.

Seymour, P. H. K. and Elder, L. (1986): Beginning reading without phonology. *Cognitive Neuropsychology*, 1, 43–82.

Seymour, P. H. K. and McGregor, C. J. (1984): Developmental dyslexia: a cognitive experimental analysis of phonological, morphemic and visual impairments. *Cognitive Neuropsychology*, 1, 43–82.

Seymour, P. H. K. and Porpodas, C. (1980): Lexical and non-lexical processing of spelling in dyslexia. In Frith, U. (ed.), *Cognitive Processes in Spelling*. London: Academic Press.

Shankweiler, D., Liberman, I. Y., Mark, L. S., Fowler, C. A and Fischer, F. W. (1979): The speech code and learning to read. *Journal of Experimental Psychology: Human Learning and Memory*, 5, 531–45.

Siegal, L. S. (1984): A longitudinal study of a hyperlexic child: hyperlexia as a language disorder. *Neuropsychologia*, 22, 577–85.

Siegal, L. S. (1985): Deep dyslexia in childhood? *Brain and Language*, 26, 16–27.

Simon, D. P. and Simon, H. A. (1973): Alternative uses of phonemic information in spelling. *Review of Educational Research*, 43, 115–37.

Simpson, G. B., Lorsbach, T. C. and Whitehouse, D. C. (1983): Encoding and contextual components of word recognition in good and poor readers. *Journal of Experimental Child Psychology*, 35, 161–71.

Snowling, M. J. (1980); The development of grapheme-phoneme correspondences in normal and dyslexic readers. *Journal of Experimental Child Psychology*, 29, 294–305.

Snowling, M. J. (1981): Phonemic deficits in developmental dyslexia. *Psychological Research*, 43, 219–34.

Snowling, M. (1982): The spelling of nasal clusters by dyslexic and normal children. *Spelling Progress Bulletin*, 22, 13–18.

Snowling, M. J. (1983): The comparison of acquired and developmental disorders of reading. *Cognition*, 14, 105–18.

Snowling, M. J. (1985): *Children's Written Language Difficulties* Windsor: NFER-Nelson.

Snowling, M. and Frith, U. (1981): The role of sound, shape and orthographic cues in early reading. *British Journal of Psychology*, 72, 83–7.

Snowling, M. and Frith, U. (1986): Comprehension in 'hyperlexic' readers. *Journal of Experimental Child Psychology*, 42, 392–415.

Snowling, M. J. and Perin, D. (1983): The development of phoneme segmentation skill in young children. In Rogers, D. A. and Sloboda, J. A. (eds), *Acquisition of Symbolic Skills*. New York: Plenum Press.

Snowling, M. J. and Stackhouse, J. (1983): Spelling performance of children with developmental verbal dyspraxia. *Developmental Medicine and Child Neurology*, 25, 430–37.

Snowling, M. J., Stackhouse, J. and Rack, J. P. (1986a): Phonological dyslexia and dysgraphia: a developmental analysis. *Cognitive Neuropsychology*, 3, 309–39.

Snowling, M. J., Goulandris, N., Bowlby, M. and Howell, P. (1986b): Segmentation and speech perception in relation to reading skill: a developmental analysis. *Journal of Experimental Child Psychology*, 41, 489–507.

Spring, C. and Capps, C. (1976): Encoding speed, rehearsal and probed recall of dyslexic boys. *Journal of Educational Psychology*, 66, 780–6.

Stanley, G. (1975): Two-part stimulus integration and specific reading disability. *Perceptual and Motor Skills*, 41, 873–4.

Stanovich, K. E. (1980): Toward an interactive-compensatory model of individual differences in the development of reading fluency. *Reading Research Quarterly*, 16, 32–71.

Stanovich, K. E., Cunningham, A. E. and Cramer, B. B. (1984): Assessing phonological awareness in kindergarten children: issues of task comparability. *Journal of Experimental Child Psychology*, 38, 175–90.

Stanovich, K. E., West, R. F. and Feeman, D. J. (1981): A longitudinal study of sentence context effects in second grade children: tests of an interactive compensatory model. *Journal of Experimental Child Psychology*, 32, 185–99.

Stuart, M. (1986): Phoneme awareness, letter-sound knowledge and learning to read. Unpublished PhD thesis, University of London.

Swanson, H. L. (1984): Semantic and visual memory codes in learning disabled readers. *Journal of Experimental Child Psychology*, 37, 124–40.

Sweeney, J. E. and Rourke, B. P. (1978): Neuropsychological significance of phonetically accurate and phonetically inaccurate spelling errors in younger and older retarded spellers. *Brain and Language*, 6, 212–25.

Taft, M. (1982): An alternative to grapheme-phoneme conversion rules? *Memory and Cognition*, 10, 465–74.

Temple, C. M. (1986): Developmental dysgraphias. *Quarterly Journal of Experimental Psychology*, 38A, 77–110.

Temple, C. and Marshall, J. C. (1983): A case study of developmental phonological dyslexia. *British Journal of Psychology*, 74, 517–33.

Thomson, M. E. (1981): An analysis of spelling errors in dyslexic children. *First Language*, 1, 141–50.

Thomson, M. E. (1982): The assessment of children with specific reading difficulties (dyslexia) using the British Ability Scales. *British Journal of Psychology*, 73, 461–78.

Thomson, M. E. (1984): *Developmental Dyslexia*. London: Lawrence Erlbaum Ass.

Treiman, R. (1984a): On the status of final consonants in English syllables. *Journal of Verbal Learning and Verbal Behaviour*, 23, 343–56.

Treiman, R. (1984b): Individual differences between children in reading and spelling styles. *Journal of Experimental Child Psychology*, 37, 463–77.

Treiman, R. (1985a): Onsets and rimes as units of spoken syllables: evidence from children. *Journal of Experimental Child Psychology*, 39, 161–81.

Treiman, R. (1985b): Phonemic awareness, spelling and reading. In Carr, T. (ed.), *New Directions in Child Development: the development of reading skills*. San Francisco: Jossey-Boss.

Treiman, R. and Hirsh-Pasek, K. (1985): Are there qualitative differences in reading behaviour between dyslexics and normal readers? *Memory and Cognition*, 13, 357–64.

van der Wessel, A. and Zegers, F. E. (1985): Reading retardation revisited. *British Journal of Developmental Psychology*, 3, 3–19.

Vellutino, F. R. (1977): Alternative conceptualization of dyslexia: evidence in support of a verbal deficit hypothesis. *Harvard Educational Review*, 47, 334–54.

Vellutino, F. R. (1979): *Dyslexia: theory and research.* Cambridge, MA.: M.I.T. Press.

Vellutino, F. R. and Scanlon, D. M. (1985): Free recall of concrete and abstract words in poor and normal readers. *Journal of Experimental Child Psychology*, 39, 363–80.

Vellutino, F. R., Pruzek, R., Steger, J. A. and Meshoulam, U. (1973): Immediate visual recall in poor readers as a function of orthographic-linguistic familiarity. *Cortex*, 9, 368–84.

West, R. F. and Stanovich, K. E. (1978): Automatic contextual facilitation in readers of three ages. *Child Development*, 49, 717–27.

Whitehouse, D. and Harris, J. C. (1984): Hyperlexia in infantile autism. *Journal of Autism and Developmental Disorders*, 14, 281–9.

Williams, R., Ingham, R. J. and Rosenthal, J. (1981): A further analysis for developmental apraxia of speech in children with defective articulation. *Journal of Speech and Hearing Research*, 24, 496–505.

Yule, W. (1967): Predicting reading ages on Neale's Analysis of Reading Ability. *British Journal of Educational Psychology*, 37, 252–5.

Yule, W., Lansdown, R. and Urbanowicz, M. A. (1982): Predicting educational attainment from W.I.S.C.-R. in a primary school sample. *British Jounal of Psychology*, 21, 43–6.

Yule, W., Rutter, M., Berger, M. and Thompson, J. (1974): Over and under achievement in reading: distribution in the general population. *British Journal of Educational Psychology*, 44, 1–11.

Index